ABCs

OF CHRISTIANITY

AN OUTLINE FOR LIVING IN THE "NOW" AND RELATING TO GOD

TERDEMA USSERY

Faith
Words

NEW YORK • BOSTON • NASHVILLE

FaithWords
Hachette Book Group
1290 Avenue of the Americas
New York, NY 10104
faithwords.com
twitter.com/faithwords

First Edition: June 2016

FaithWords is a division of Hachette Book Group, Inc.
The FaithWords name and logo are trademarks of Hachette Book Group, Inc.

The publisher is not responsible for websites (or their content) that are not owned by the publisher.

The Hachette Speakers Bureau provides a wide range of authors for speaking events. To find out more, go to www.hachettespeakersbureau.com or call (866) 376-6591.

ISBNs: 978-1-4555-3780-8 (hardcover), 978-1-4555-3779-2 (ebook)

Printed in the United States of America

RRD-C

10 9 8 7 6 5 4 3 2 1

CONTENTS

Foreword   *v*

Acknowledgments   *vii*

Introduction   *ix*

How to Use This Book and Your Bible   *xiii*

God   *1*

The Bible   *7*

Jesus   *13*

The Holy Spirit   *23*

Satan   *31*

Sin   *33*

Repentance   *43*

The Church   *49*

Baptism and Communion (The Lord's Supper)   *67*

Death   *71*

Judgment of the Nations and the Wicked   *77*

Salvation vs. Rewards   *81*

Prayer   *87*

Faith   *99*

The Abundant Life   *107*

The New Birth   *111*

God's Plan of Salvation   *113*

Glossary   *119*

About the Author   *143*

With Gratitude from a Believing Son   *145*

Notes   *155*

FOREWORD

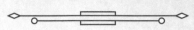

Dr. Terdema Ussery and his wife, Jean, have together been an inspiration and role model to our family the past thirty years. For as long as we have known them, Terdema and Jean graciously opened their home to a weekly Tuesday night Bible study entitled "The ABCs of Christianity." This Bible study fostered our growth and understanding of our Lord and Savior, Jesus Christ. These enriched classes included not only biblical knowledge, fellowship with the saints, and a spiritual worship experience but also endless refreshments and hospitality.

When Pastor Ussery became the interim pastor of our church, his abilities to lead were highlighted. Under his pastorate the church tripled in size and programs were instituted, supported, and performed with fidelity. There was a sense of enthusiasm for the Word and the work of our Savior, Jesus Christ. Morale was at an all-time high! He gave life to old bones.

His dedicated teaching of the ABCs of Christianity is well-known throughout the United Church of Christ community. Now that this book is published, it will be useful to many—clergy and laymen!

Patricia A. Mattison, M.A.,
and Charles A. Mattison, D.D.S., D.Min.

ACKNOWLEDGMENTS

I want to thank the following persons for their help and insight in preparing this book: The Tuesday-night Bible study class, whose thirst for the scriptures kept me digging and searching through the Bible for deeper understanding. Minister Terdema Ussery II, for using his editing skills, developed partially as a former executive editor of the *California Law Review,* to take over the document and bring it to fruition. I want to thank him for his patience. Adrienne Ingrum, of Hachette Book Group, for her editorial assistance. Jan Miller, of Dupree/Miller and Associates, who is my literary agent.

Finally, I would like to thank my wife, Jean Ussery. She is the person who encouraged me to take this journey of Bible teaching, and what a journey it has been! She is my life partner and has accompanied me every step of the way. She is truly the wind beneath my wings.

Pastor Ussery

INTRODUCTION

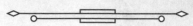

Many people think you need to study Christianity to have a relationship with God. However, just because you studied something and committed it to memory does not mean you understand it and can practice it in your life. You need to study more deeply than that. Studying the Bible—its structure, simplicities, perplexities, and analogies—gives you the skills that are necessary to have a relationship with God. A divine and innate presence is in all of us. Yet until you wake up to the essential meaning of the Bible, you will continue to live outside yourself, searching for a higher power.

I have lived my life with an intuitive reverence for God. I know for sure that there is not a place on earth where God does not exist. I have experienced tumultuous times as well as moments of enthusiasm, and in all of them, I have been met with the presence of God.

I take great delight, pleasure, gratification, and enjoyment in writing what I have learned on my well-lived spiritual journey. I've been looking back through my mind's eye since the precious age of six.

I was born on a cold day in August 1931. Some may say that I entered life without the likelihood to thrive. I emerged from the womb at seven months and was fed sweet potatoes from the end of my grandmother's finger. The positive energy and love from my grandmother allowed me to sprout into a healthy boy. I grew up on a ninety-acre farm, where I gave myself to Christ at the age of twelve while attending our neighborhood Providence AME Church, in Gurdon, Arkansas.

My early relationship with God allowed me to see myself as a part of God's great scheme. My relationship with God allowed me to honor the fact that I am a "jack of all trades, master of none." If you need carpentry work, electrical wiring, a needle threaded, or a blueprint made, I can do it. I am attuned to the collection of physical gifts God has bestowed on me, and with the spiritual gifts as well. The spiritual insights God has seen fit to give me in my experiences along life's way I now call lessons—or ABCs.

I was first compelled to share these lessons in 1975, when my wife, Jean, and a group of women asked me to teach a Bible study class. My initial response was, "I do not want to teach a women-only group."

Jean said, "Everyone thinks you teach the Bible the best," and asked, "Would you do it for me?"

Well, that was the end of the conversation. I did it.

This handbook represents the centerpiece of my life,

the most introspective look at the two things that matter most to me in life:

- Living in the "now." All we really have is right now.

- Having a personal relationship with God. Nothing is more valuable in life than having a relationship with God.

May this book be of service to you who want to live in the now and actively know God. All is joy in knowing and believing.

The outline format of this book has great advantages over wordy, preachy books. This book is meant to be used along with your Bible, Internet Bible site, or Bible app—whichever translation or version you prefer. Those who are reading or teaching may use this book as an outline to which they can add more detail.

Pastor Terdema Ussery, J.D., MM.

HOW TO USE THIS BOOK AND YOUR BIBLE

This book is a basic outline of Christian beliefs. You may use this book with any Bible translation you choose. I explain terms that may be unfamiliar to you in the glossary on page 119, but you may also want to use your own Bible dictionary. I use no abbreviations for the sixty-six books that make up the Bible, but your Bible app might, so below is a list of the sixty-six books with commonly used abbreviations for them.

BOOK NAME	ABBREVIATIONS
Genesis	Gen, Ge, Gn
Exodus	Exo, Ex, Exod
Leviticus	Lev, Le, Lv
Numbers	Num, Nu, Nm, Nb
Deuteronomy	Deut, Dt
Joshua	Josh, Jos, Jsh
Judges	Judg, Jdg, Jg, Jdgs
Ruth	Rth, Ru

BOOK NAME	ABBREVIATIONS
1 Samuel	1 Sam, 1 Sa, 1Samuel, 1S, I Sa, 1 Sm, 1Sa, I Sam, 1Sam, I Samuel, 1st Samuel, First Samuel
2 Samuel	2 Sam, 2 Sa, 2S, II Sa, 2 Sm, 2Sa, II Sam, 2Sam, II Samuel, 2Samuel, 2nd Samuel, Second Samuel
1 Kings	1 Kgs, 1 Ki, 1K, I Kgs, 1Kgs, I Ki, 1Ki, I Kings, 1Kings, 1st Kgs, 1st Kings, First Kings, First Kgs, 1Kin
2 Kings	2 Kgs, 2 Ki, 2K, II Kgs, 2Kgs, II Ki, 2Ki, II Kings, 2Kings, 2nd Kgs, 2nd Kings, Second Kings, Second Kgs, 2Kin
1 Chronicles	1 Chron, 1 Ch, I Ch, 1Ch, 1 Chr, I Chr, 1Chr, I Chron, 1Chron, I Chronicles, 1Chronicles, 1st Chronicles, First Chronicles
2 Chronicles	2 Chron, 2 Ch, II Ch, 2Ch, II Chr, 2Chr, II Chron, 2Chron, II Chronicles, 2Chronicles, 2nd Chronicles, Second Chronicles
Ezra	Ezra, Ezr
Nehemiah	Neh, Ne
Esther	Esth, Es
Job	Job, Job, Jb
Psalm	Pslm, Ps, Psalms, Psa, Psm, Pss
Proverbs	Prov, Pr, Prv
Ecclesiastes	Eccles, Ec, Ecc, Qoh, Qoheleth
Song of Solomon	Song, So, Canticle of Canticles, Canticles, Song of Songs, SOS
Isaiah	Isa, Is
Jeremiah	Jer, Je, Jr

BOOK NAME	ABBREVIATIONS
Lamentations	Lam, La
Ezekiel	Ezek, Eze, Ezk
Daniel	Dan, Da, Dn
Hosea	Hos, Ho
Joel	Joel, Joe, Jl
Amos	Amos, Am
Obadiah	Obad, Ob
Jonah	Jnh, Jon
Micah	Micah, Mic
Nahum	Nah, Na
Habakkuk	Hab, Hab
Zephaniah	Zeph, Zep, Zp
Haggai	Haggai, Hag, Hg
Zechariah	Zech, Zec, Zc
Malachi	Mal, Mal, Ml
Matthew	Matt, Mt
Mark	Mrk, Mk, Mr
Luke	Luk, Lk
John	John, Jn, Jhn
Acts	Acts, Ac
Romans	Rom, Ro, Rm
1 Corinthians	1 Cor, 1 Co, I Co, 1Co, I Cor, 1Cor, I Corinthians, 1Corinthians, 1st Corinthians, First Corinthians
2 Corinthians	2 Cor, 2 Co, II Co, 2Co, II Cor, 2Cor, II Corinthians, 2Corinthians, 2nd Corinthians, Second Corinthians

BOOK NAME	ABBREVIATIONS
Galatians	Gal, Ga
Ephesians	Ephes, Eph
Philippians	Phil, Php
Colossians	Col, Col
1 Thessalonians	1 Thess, 1 Th, I Th, 1Th, I Thes, 1Thes, I Thess, 1Thess, I Thessalonians, 1Thessalonians, 1st Thessalonians, First Thessalonians
2 Thessalonians	2 Thess, 2 Th, II Th, 2Th, II Thes, 2Thes, II Thess, 2Thess, II Thessalonians, 2Thessalonians, 2nd Thessalonians, Second Thessalonians
1 Timothy	1 Tim, 1 Ti, I Ti, 1Ti, I Tim, 1Tim, I Timothy, 1Timothy, 1st Timothy, First Timothy
2 Timothy	2 Tim, 2 Ti, II Ti, 2Ti, II Tim, 2Tim, II Timothy, 2Timothy, 2nd Timothy, Second Timothy
Titus	Titus, Tit
Philemon	Philem, Phm
Hebrews	Hebrews, Heb
James	James, Jas, Jm
1 Peter	1 Pet, 1 Pe, I Pe, 1Pe, I Pet, 1Pet, I Pt, 1 Pt, 1Pt, I Peter, 1Peter, 1st Peter, First Peter
2 Peter	2 Pet, 2 Pe, II Pe, 2Pe, II Pet, 2Pet, II Pt, 2 Pt, 2Pt, II Peter, 2Peter, 2nd Peter, Second Peter
1 John	1 John, 1 Jn, I Jn, 1Jn, I Jo, 1Jo, I Joh, 1Joh, I Jhn, 1 Jhn, 1Jhn, I John, 1John, 1st John, First John
2 John	2 John, 2 Jn, II Jn, 2Jn, II Jo, 2Jo, II Joh, 2Joh, II Jhn, 2 Jhn, 2Jhn, II John, 2John, 2nd John, Second John

BOOK NAME	ABBREVIATIONS
3 John	3 John, 3 Jn, III Jn, 3Jn, III Jo, 3Jo, III Joh, 3Joh, III Jhn, 3 Jhn, 3Jhn, III John, 3John, 3rd John, Third John
Jude	Jude, Jud
Revelation	Rev, Re, The Revelation

Logos, *Bible Book Name Abbreviations, https://www.logos.com/support /windows/L3/book_abbreviations*

Let's Decode Bible Book Chapters and Verses

Each of the sixty-six books of the Bible is broken into chapters and verses, except one. The exception is Philemon. That book has only one chapter, so it contains only verses.

John 3:16, for example, means the book of John, chapter 3, verse 16. When I provide the name of a Bible book with its chapter and verse, find the verse using your Bible or your preferred Internet Bible site or your Bible app. Read the verse carefully. What the Bible says is more important than what I say. This book is only a guide to help you draw out the meaning of the Bible. My goal is to help you make sense of what the Bible says and apply it to your own life.

It can be confusing to find some of the books of the Bible because quite a few have the same name. Only the number in front of the name lets you tell them apart.

1 Samuel	2 John
2 Samuel	3 John
1 Kings	1 Thessalonians
2 Kings	2 Thessalonians
1 Chronicles	1 Timothy
2 Chronicles	2 Timothy
John	1 Peter
1 John	2 Peter

How to Choose a Bible or Bible App

If you use a smartphone, tablet, e-book reader, or laptop you have a wide choice of Bibles available in your "app store" and many are free. Choose any one you like. Make sure you learn how to access the Bible when you are offline—not connected to the Internet.

Whether you choose to read the Bible on an app, on the Internet, or on paper, you will have to select a translation. As you'll learn in the chapter entitled "The Bible," the Bible was not written in English. It was written in ancient languages that have to be translated into languages we understand. The King James Version (KJV) was an English translation completed in 1611, more than four hundred years ago. While it *is* in English, it's not in the English we speak today. And while many think the "thees" and "thous" of the KJV mean it is the *real* Bible, this is simply not true. Other translations that use current, easily understood English more accurately reflect those ancient Bible scrolls. So, choose a Bible translation that you can read and understand easily.

Christians sometimes argue the merits of one translation versus another. These arguments are usually based on denominations or people's beliefs on specific religious subjects. Don't get caught up in these arguments. *ABCs of Christianity* is meant to foster your relationship with the God of the Bible. Pick up whatever Bible you have and let's go meet God!

GOD

The Bible nowhere attempts to prove the existence of God. The Old and New Testament writers took the existence of God for granted. The Bible begins with the fact that God is. You may say you "just know" God exists or "can just feel" God. Others say they sense God in the wind, in natural beauty, or the awe and orderliness of the universe. Yet others say they see God in people, in their love, compassion, and kind acts. Any argument of the Almighty's existence would be inconclusive. We will not argue; we will start by just saying, "God is."

GOD IS THE ONLY INFINITE AND ETERNAL BEING

God has no beginning and no end.
Genesis 1:1–2, Revelation 1:8

God is the creator and sustainer of all things.
Colossians 1:16–17, John 1:3, 1 Corinthians 8:6

God is the supreme personal intelligence.
Colossians 2:3

God is the righteous ruler of the universe.
Deuteronomy 4:39, 1 Chronicles 29:12

God is life, and, therefore, the only source of life.
Job 33:4

God is alive and true, in contrast to lifeless idols and the whole false system of idolatry. *Psalm 96:4–6.* We live in a society that idolizes those who idolize themselves!

God can be known through the Bible.
2 Timothy 3:16–17

- By prophets in the Old Testament *Hebrews 1:1*

- Through Jesus Christ in the New Testament *Hebrews 1:2*

GOD HAS A PERSONALITY

God's personality is expressed in many ways:
God loves. *John 3:16*
God hates. *Proverbs 6:16*
God cares. *1 Peter 5:7*
God grieves. *Genesis 6:6*

Only a personality can do the above. Therefore, God must be a personal being.

God's Nature

God is beyond human comprehension, so the following nine aspects of God found in the Bible are incomplete, but they do give us an indication of the nature of God:

The nature of God is expressed in divine compassion. *Psalm 103:13*

There is no evil in God, only good. *1 John 1:5, Psalm 92:15*

God is holy. *Leviticus 11:44–45*

God is a spirit—God's divine essence. *John 4:24*

God can be present with us. *Genesis 3:8*

God can communicate with us. *Exodus 3:4–5, 1 Kings 19:11–13, John 10:27*

God has all knowledge. *Psalm 33:13–15, 147:5*

God holds all power. *Revelation 19:6*

God is present everywhere. *Psalm 139:7–10*

True or false: If God is everywhere present, we can worship any object.

False: God is everywhere but God is not *in* everything. God is spirit, and those who worship God must worship in spirit and in truth. *John 4:24*

THE GRACE OF GOD

Grace is the love and mercy of God in action.
Ephesians 2:8–9, Lamentations 3:22, Psalm 103:8

Love is a positive force that generates from a perfect God.

Mercy is the mitigation a perfect God extends toward the negative force of human sin.

Taken together, they make grace: Mercy + Love = Grace.

God's grace is unconditional and forever.
Romans 8:38–39

It is not given on the condition that we hold out until the end.

It is not given on the condition that we do the right things.

It is not given on the condition that we succeed or do not fail.

It is not given on the condition that we do our best.

God's grace is all we need, no matter what our failings. *2 Corinthians 12:9*

All are invited to partake of God's grace. *Titus 2:11*

The grace of God justifies—declares not guilty, acquits in the court of heaven. (This happens when we are saved.) *Romans 3:23–24*

God's grace makes every believer an heir to eternal life. *Titus 3:7, John 1:12*

The grace of God teaches believers to deny ungodliness and worldly lusts, to live soberly, and be moderate, in control. *Titus 2:11–12*

What is grace then?

It is the unlimited love of God expressed in the gift of God's Son, Jesus, who is our Savior.

It is the undeserved love of God toward all of us who do the wrong things.

THE TRINITY OF GOD

"Trinity" mean God's existence as three distinct persons in one God. Think of water. Water can be liquid, solid (ice), or gas (steam). Water can take three forms, but in each form it is water. The Bible refers to God as Father, Son, and Holy Spirit.

- Father—invisible, sent Jesus Christ, heads the divine Trinity *1 Peter 1:2–3, John 1:18, John 14:28*

- Jesus Christ—the Son, God manifested in the flesh *Hebrews 1:8, John 1:14*

- Holy Spirit—God in action on humanity *Ezekiel 36:27*

We can also think of God as Creator, Redeemer, and Spirit.

God reveals to us our sin. *John 16:7–11*

God guides believers into all truths. *John 16:12–15*

The Trinity is not explicit in the Old Testament. It is only implied in plural statements such as "Let us make man." *Genesis 1:26 KJV.* "Us" means more than one. The Trinity is revealed in the New Testament.

Matthew 3:16–17

Christ is baptized in water.

The Father speaks from heaven.

The Holy Spirit descends like a dove.

In the name of all three persons we are to be baptized.

Look at the Trinity like your human body/soul/spirit. *1 Thessalonians 5:23.* In the Trinity is one God—Father, Son, and Holy Spirit—in perfect unity. *1 John 5:6–8.*

THE BIBLE

The Bible is the only Word of the living God that we have. No other book makes this claim. The Bible is not philosophy, although it is philosophical. The Bible is not a scientific treatise, yet there are no discrepancies between certain facts of science and the Bible. The Bible is not a book of history, yet it is accurate when recording history. The Bible is the only book that throws light on or into past and future eternities. The Bible is a *now* book—spoken to us by a *now* God. How far is it from earth to heaven? That is the height the Bible is above all other books.

The Bible contains sixty-six books from thirty-five credited writers, written in Hebrew, Greek, and Aramaic over a period of fifteen hundred years. Its subjects include religion, history, law, science, poetry, drama, biography, autobiography, and prophecy. The writers represent a cross section of humanity: educated and uneducated, farmers and kings, fishermen and doctors, teachers and public officials. All the writers were the same in these respects: All were moved by God's Spirit, all uttered things beyond their knowledge, and all searched diligently for the meaning of the words they were given. The various books of the Bible are as harmoniously united as the parts that make up the human body.

The Bible should always be read with an ear tuned, listening for the voice of God, for only through the Bible can we hear the Almighty speak to us as our Father. It has been said of the Bible: Read it to be wise. Believe it to be safe. Practice it to be right.

CHRIST IS THE CENTER OF THE BIBLE

The Old Testament points forward to Jesus. The New Testament points back to Jesus. He is the circumference of the Bible. The Bible reveals Christ from Genesis to Revelation. *John 5:39*

THE BIBLE CLAIMS TO BE THE INSPIRED WORD OF GOD

Not just some of the Bible but the entire Bible is the inspired Word of God. *2 Timothy 3:16–17*

"Inspired" means God's Spirit supernaturally influenced the writers. The Scriptures of God are inspired, word for word. Every word is equally inspired. Therefore, the Bible does not only contain the Word of God; it *is* the Word of God. God's Spirit is the author of the Bible.

Men were used by God's Spirit to write the Bible. *2 Peter 1:20–21*

The Bible is absolutely trustworthy and free from error in its original form. *Psalm 119:160, Proverbs 30:5*

The Bible is eternal. *Matthew 24:35*

The Bible Is a Difficult Book

It is difficult because it came from unlimited, all-powerful God to limited man, from the infinite (God) to the finite (man), from the spiritual (God) to the natural (man). *1 Corinthians 2:14–16*

We cannot understand the Bible as we would the writings of Plato or Aristotle. By study and diligent application, we are able to grasp the profound meaning of writers such as Plato and Aristotle. Natural man understands natural books. But we cannot understand the Bible on our own; it is not a natural book. We can only apply our limited natural reasoning. Because the Bible is a spiritual book given by God, to understand the Bible and its teaching we must have the mind of Christ—be no longer controlled by the natural mind but rather by God's Spirit. *Philippians 2:2–5*

Then the Bible is not difficult.

Read the Bible prayerfully, asking that God's Spirit teach and guide you to understanding. If not, it will remain a difficult, closed book to you. *John 16:12–15*

The Bible Claims Special Powers

The Bible has special powers. *Hebrews 4:12*

The Bible has the power to divide like a sword. The Bible will separate man from sin and sin can separate man from the Bible. *Psalm 119:11, Isaiah 59:2*

The Bible has the power to reflect as a mirror. In the Bible we see ourselves as God sees us. *James 1:22–25*

The Bible has the power to cleanse like water. The Bible purifies. *Ephesians 5:26*

The Bible has the power to reproduce like a seed. The Bible shows us how to become spiritually alive.
1 Peter 1:23, John 3:17

The Bible has the power to nourish our spirit. The Bible is spiritual food for the soul. *1 Peter 2:2*

No Christian can remain strong in the Lord if he or she does not study the Word of God.

THE BIBLE COMMANDS THE BELIEVER TO STUDY THE SCRIPTURES

The believer must study the Scriptures. *2 Timothy 2:15*

Be diligent in your study of the Bible so you can work for God without shame. Equip yourself completely so you may handle God's Word of truth accurately and be able to give the true meaning to those you teach or who seek answers. To become a better Christian, look at the Scriptures in terms of its application to your life. Most times we look at the Scriptures to find fault in someone else. When studying the Scriptures, remember: God is true and cannot lie, and man is natural and is therefore limited.

> *For the word of God is living and active and sharper than any two-edged sword, and piercing as far as the division of soul and spirit, of both joints and marrow, and able to judge the thoughts and intentions of the heart.*
>
> *Hebrews 4:12 NASB*

JESUS

[J]esus is a real historical figure. That Jesus lived has been proved by historians, not just by the Bible. Christianity differs from all other religions because it holds that Jesus was born as the sinless human Son of God. With God the Creator and God the Spirit, Jesus forms the Trinity—the divine Godhead. Jesus is the subject of or tangent to every book in the New Testament.

THE GOD NATURE OF JESUS

Jesus is an eternal being referred to in the Bible book of John as "the Word." *John 1:1*

Jesus was both with God *and* was God. *John 1:1–3*

Jesus is the creator and maker of all things. *Colossians 1:16*

Jesus is the sustainer of all things. *Hebrews 1:3*

Jesus received worship by those who knew that only God is to be worshipped. *Matthew 14:33, Acts 10:25–26*

Jesus claimed to have all authority in heaven and on earth after his resurrection. *Matthew 28:18*

Jesus forgave sin, knowing only God has the power to forgive sin. *Mark 2:5–11*

The Bible records more than twenty miracles performed by Jesus. To name just a few: He walked on the water of the Sea of Galilee; wind and waves obeyed His command; He healed the sick and brought the dead back to life on earth; He cast out demons and made the crippled walk; He turned water into wine; and with the lunch of one boy, He fed more than five thousand people. *John 21:25*

THE HUMAN NATURE OF JESUS CHRIST

Jesus was human and was declared to be the Son of God. *Romans 1:3–4*

Jesus was from the Jewish lineage of King David. *Matthew 1:6–17*

Jesus' birth mother, Mary, was a virgin. *Luke 1:34–35*

Jesus experienced life as a human being, feeling

- Hunger *Matthew 4:2*

- Thirst *John 19:28*

- Fatigue *John 4:6*

- Sorrow *John 11:35*

- Temptation *Hebrews 4:15*

Note: Temptation is not sin. It is not wrong to feel tempted.

THE VIRGIN BIRTH OF JESUS CHRIST

Jesus Christ was born with two natures: God and Human.

Jesus was born of a virgin. *Luke 1:26–35*

We find the first hint of the virgin birth in *Genesis 3:15*, where it is foretold that the one to defeat Satan was to be born of the seed of a woman. We understand this to mean that no human father was involved. Only God can consummate life from a seed. Mary had never experienced a sexual relationship with a man, yet she bore a son. It was thought to be impossible then. Today, it is not thought of as impossible. We call it artificial insemination.

Christ was born free from sin in order to redeem humans from sin.

Because of Adam's sin, humans are born with a sinful nature. *Genesis 3, Romans 3:23*

THE DEATH OF JESUS CHRIST

The death of Jesus Christ is mentioned more than 120 times in the New Testament alone. It is also spoken of prophetically many times in the Old Testament. The death of Jesus is recorded in all four gospels: *Matthew 27:45–50, Mark 15:33–37, Luke 23:44–46, John 19:28–30*

Jesus died a martyr's death. *Philippians 2:8*

Because Jesus lived a sinless life, His death replaced the death of all humans for all times. No one has to die because of sin. Jesus was a substitute for sinners. *2 Corinthians 5:21* Jesus' death was a sin offering for all humanity.

The death of Jesus was *natural. John 19:31–37.* This means that His spirit and soul separated from His body. He experienced a physical death. Jesus literally died.

The death of Jesus was *unnatural. Romans 6:23.* Death was the curse on sinners after the fall of Adam. But since Jesus had no sin, He did not have to die. Before Jesus could die, He had to take on sins. He took on our sin, He allowed himself to die on our behalf; therefore He was no longer sinless, although He Himself had committed no sin.

The death of Jesus was *preternatural. Revelation 13:8.* Jesus' death was not an accident, not unexpected; it was predetermined by God. *Isaiah 53:5*

The circumstances of the death of Jesus were *super-*

natural. John 10:17–18. Jesus laid down His life. It was not taken from Him. He laid it down by his own initiative. He had supernatural power and authority from God the Father to take it up again.

Eyewitness Accounts of the Resurrection of Jesus Christ

An empty tomb (grave) and linen wrapping (grave clothes) were found where Jesus' body was buried. *John 20:1–10*

The Bible records these reports that Jesus was alive again three days after he was killed:

- Mary Magdalene saw Him. *John 20:11–18*

- The disciples saw Him when they were on the road to Emmaus. *Luke 24:13–33*

- Peter saw Him. *Luke 24:34*

- All the apostles, except one, Thomas, saw Him. *Luke 24:36–43*

- All the apostles, along with Thomas, saw Him. *John 20:26–29*

- More than five hundred followers saw Him. *1 Corinthians 15:6*

- Stephen, the first Christian martyr, saw Him. *Acts 7:55*

Close followers of Jesus fled when Jesus was arrested. *Matthew 26:55*

They did not believe Jesus would come back to life after He was killed. *John 20:9*

When Jesus died, they were dejected, discouraged, and defeated. Three days later they had an attitude adjustment when they saw Jesus alive again. They touched the resurrected Jesus. They ate with Him. He was fully alive and human. He bore the scars where the nails had pierced His hands and feet. *John 20:26*

Many of these eyewitnesses died martyr deaths because they preached the resurrection of Jesus Christ. They were glad to die for a living Christ (Savior). They had the proof of the resurrection, and it was convincing. It was the beginning of the Christian religion.

The lives of the disciples changed. Upon Jesus' arrest, they fled. But after the resurrection, they had unlimited courage. *Acts 5:40–42*

The early Church worshipped on the first day of the week, rather than the Jewish tradition of the last day of the week. It was a spontaneous response to the resurrection of Jesus on the first day of the week. *Acts 20:7*

Early Christians went everywhere telling of the resurrection of Jesus, that He came back to life after dying. *Acts 8:1–4*

THE ASCENSION AND SECOND COMING OF JESUS CHRIST

After forty days of instructing His disciples, the risen Christ ascended bodily on a literal cloud. His ascension was visible. *Acts 1:1–9*

Jesus' return to earth is prophesied. Two angels brought the message of this second coming to those who watched as Jesus was ascending to heaven. *Acts 1:10–11*

His return to earth will be actual, bodily, literally visible using our eyes, and on the exact spot and place where he ascended from the Mount of Olives, in what is now Israel. (He will not come to America, *Zechariah 14:4, Acts 1:12.*) The second coming of Jesus is mentioned more than three hundred times in the New Testament. *Matthew 25:31–46*

He is coming for the following reasons:

- To take His followers (the Church) to be with Him. *John 14:1–3*

- To judge the nations. *Matthew 25:31–46*

- To save Israel. *Romans 11:25–26*

- To sit on the throne of David. *Luke 1:31–33*

- To bring righteous government to the earth. *Hebrews 1:8*

Jesus is now seated at the right hand of God, the Father. *Hebrews 10:12*

Jesus is the "Son" in the Trinity. *Matthew 16:14–15*

Jesus is the head of the long train of biblical heroes. *Hebrews 11*

He is the author and finisher of our faith. Every part of His life and conduct is an example for us. *Hebrews 12:1–2*

Jesus is the following to believers:

- A helper, an advocate *1 John 2:1*

- The righteous one, the just one who suffered for us, the unjust *Romans 5:8*

- The anointed sacrifice—for sin *1 John 2:2*

Christ is Christianity, and Christianity is Christ.

> *Yet for us there is one God, the Father,* from
> *whom are all things and for whom we exist,*
> *and one Lord, Jesus Christ,* through *whom*
> *are all things and through whom we exist.*
>
> *1 Corinthians 8:6 NLT*

THE FULFILLMENT OF PROPHECY

Forty-four Old Testament prophesies regarding the Messiah were fulfilled by Jesus. Here are some of them:

- The Messiah would be born in Bethlehem. Micah 5:2 *(Matthew 2:1; Luke 2:4-6)*

- The Messiah would be born of a virgin. Isaiah 7:14 *(Matthew 1:22-23; Luke 1:26-31)*

- The Messiah would come from the line of Abraham. Genesis 12:3; Genesis 22:18 *(Matthew 1:1; Romans 9:5)*

- The Messiah would be heir to King David's throne. 2 Samuel 7:12-13; Isaiah 9:7 *(Luke 1:32-33; Romans 1:3)*

- The Messiah's throne will be anointed and eternal. Psalm 45:6-7; Daniel 2:44 *(Luke 1:33; Hebrews 1:8-12)*

- A messenger would prepare the way for the Messiah, as foretold in Isaiah 40:3-5 *(Luke 3:3-6)*

- The Messiah would be rejected by his own people, as foretold in Psalm 69:8; Isaiah 53:3 *(John 1:11; John 7:5)*

- The Messiah would be declared the Son of God, as foretold in Psalm 2:7 *(Matthew 3:16-17)*

- The Messiah would be sent to heal the brokenhearted, as foretold in Isaiah 61:1-2 *(Luke 4:18-19)*

- The Messiah would be betrayed, as foretold in Psalm 41:9; Zechariah 11:12-13 *(Luke 22:47-48; Matthew 26:14-16)*

- The Messiah would be falsely accused, as foretold in Psalm 35:11 *(Mark 14:57-58)*

- The Messiah would be crucified with criminals, as foretold in Isaiah 53:12 *(Matthew 27:38; Mark 15:27-28)*

- The Messiah's hands and feet would be pierced, as foretold in Psalm 22:16; Zechariah 12:10 *(John 20:25-27)*

- The Messiah would be resurrected from the dead, as foretold in Psalm 16:10; Psalm 49:15 *(Matthew 28:2-7; Acts 2:22-32)*

- The Messiah would be seated at the right hand of God (the Father), as foretold in Psalm 68:18; Psalm 110:1 *(Mark 16:19; Matthew 22:44)*

- The Messiah would be a sacrifice for sin, as foretold in Isaiah 53:5-12 *(Romans 5:6-8)*

THE HOLY SPIRIT

T he Holy Spirit is the Spirit of God. He is set forth in the Bible as distinct from and equal to God the Father and God the Son.

The Holy Spirit is the third divine presence in the Trinity. Named as equal to the Father and the Son in two important Christian activities: the baptism of believers as part of the Great Commission (*Matthew 28:19*) and in the Apostolic Benediction following Communion. *2 Corinthians 13:14.*

THE DIVINE ATTRIBUTES OF THE HOLY SPIRIT

The Holy Spirit is everywhere present in the universe. *Psalm 139:7–10*

He has all power. *Luke 1:35*

He has all knowledge. *1 Corinthians 2:10–11*

He is eternal. *Hebrews 9:14*

The Holy Spirit in Relation to the Life and Ministry of Christ

The Holy Spirit was present in the life of Jesus.

Jesus was conceived by the Holy Spirit. *Luke 1:35*

Jesus was anointed by the Holy Spirit. *Acts 10:38*

Jesus was led by the Holy Spirit. *Matthew 4:1*

Jesus was raised from the dead by the power of the Holy Spirit. *Romans 8:11*

Jesus gave commands to the apostles through the Holy Spirit. *Acts 1:2*

Jesus was willing to die as an offering to God through the Holy Spirit. *Hebrews 9:14*

The Emblems of the Holy Spirit

Writers of the Bible used symbolic objects to describe the Holy Spirit because it is difficult to impart nonmaterial truth by the use of words. Emblems can illustrate more than thousands of words. These are the emblems that describe the Holy Spirit:

- Fire, signifying consuming and purifying power *Acts 2:3*

- Wind, signifying regenerating power *John 3:8*

- Water, signifying the power to fill to overflowing with spiritual life *John 7:37–39*

- Seal, signifying membership in the family of God *Ephesians 1:13*

- Oil, signifying the power to anoint for service *Acts 10:38*

- Dove, signifying a gentle, tender, and peaceful nature *Mark 1:10*

SINS AGAINST THE HOLY SPIRIT

To blaspheme the Holy Spirit is to make an insulting remark or curse God's Spirit. Blaspheming the Holy Spirit is unforgivable if it is done maliciously and knowingly. It is often called the unpardonable sin. Blaspheming the Holy Spirit is also attributing to Satan the works of the Holy Spirit. For example, enemies of Jesus accused him of casting out demons by the power of Satan. *Matthew 12:24 and 31–32*

Blasphemy of the Holy Spirit is committed when God's Spirit is

- Spoken of abusively *Jude 8*

- Reviled *Hebrews 10:29*

- Defamed *2 Peter 2:11*

- Slandered *Romans 3:8*

Those who reject Christ are resisting the Holy Spirit. *Acts 7:51*

When those who have accepted Christ do not give God control of their lives, they grieve the Holy Spirit. *Ephesians 4:30–32*

When believers do not confess the wrongs they know they have done, they quench the Holy Spirit. *Ephesians 6:16, 1 Thessalonians 5:19*

Believers lie to the Holy Spirit when they pretend. *Acts 5:1–11*

Ananias and Sapphira, whose names mean "grace" and "beauty," were followers of Christ, members of the Apostolic Church. They had to have had a real experience of salvation to be part of the early Church, and all who belonged were one team. Yet Ananias and Sapphira planned deception. They pretended to do what pleased God so those around them would think well of them. They lied to the Holy Spirit. *Acts 1:14, Acts 5:4*

THE WORKS OF THE HOLY SPIRIT

The Holy Spirit

- Is sent by both the Father and the Son. *John 14:16, 26*

- Is our Paraclete—Helper—on earth. *John 14:26, 15:26*

- Convinces all that unbelief is the foundation of sin. *John 16:8–9*

- Exposes unbelief as the source of sinfulness that damns. *John 3:16–20*

- Reproves our righteousness as useless and points us to Christ as our true righteousness. *John 16:10*

- Judges those who do not accept Christ. *John 16:11.* (Believers in Christ escape judgment.)

- Regenerates believers, makes them "born again." *John 3:5*

- Indwells believers. *1 Corinthians 6:19–20*

- Seals believers. *Ephesians 1:13–14*

- Baptizes believers. *Acts 1:5*

- Fills those believers who seek God for fullness of the Spirit. *Ephesians 5:18*

- Empowers believers. *Acts 1:8*

- Leads believers. We struggle when we do not
  allow the Spirit to lead. *Galatians 5:16–18*

- Administers spiritual gifts to believers.
  1 Corinthians 12:1–11

The Holy Spirit came on the day of Pentecost and
will remain until Christ comes again. Jesus finished the
work He came to do, but the Holy Spirit's work will not
be complete until Jesus returns and the Church is presented to Jesus Christ upon His return.

Followers of Jesus need the Holy Spirit to propagate
the Gospel. *John 16:7–14*

THE FRUIT OF THE HOLY SPIRIT

The fruit of the Holy Spirit is the spontaneous work of
the Holy Spirit *in believers.*

The Holy Spirit inspires agape love (divine love) in
believers. *Romans 5:1–5*

Without the love of the Spirit, believers are just religious noise. *1 Corinthians 13:1*

All the other fruits of the Holy Spirit are preceded by
love. *Galatians 5:22–23*

- Joy—love's strength, emotional excitement over blessings for yourself and others *Matthew 2:10, Acts 3:8, 1 Corinthians 13:4–7*

- Peace—love's security, peace in the midst of turmoil *Isaiah 54:10*

- Patience—love's endurance. Love does not hurry; it suffers long. *1 Corinthians 13:14*

- Kindness—love's conduct. Love is generous in action, never acts rashly. Love is not insolent, puffed up, or proud. *1 Corinthians 13:4*

- Goodness—love's character. Love is kind and virtuous, never irritated, never resentful. *1 Corinthians 13:4–5*

- Faithfulness—love's confidence. Love fully relies on God. *Psalm 9:10, Proverbs 3:5–6*

- Gentleness—love's humility, love in hiding, with no parade and no airs *Colossians 3:12; 2 Corinthians 8:7*

- Self-control—love's victory. Love is never glad when others go wrong. *Proverbs 23:1–5, 1 Corinthians 12:25–27*

THE HOLY SPIRIT SUPERSEDES THE LAW

A Spirit-controlled person needs no law to live a righteous life. *Romans 8:2*

DEDICATION IS THE SECRET OF A SPIRIT-CONTROLLED LIFE

When you offer yourself fully to God, the Holy Spirit will fill your heart with love. *Romans 5:5*

NAMES THE BIBLE USES TO REFER TO THE HOLY SPIRIT

- Fire *Acts 2:3*

- Wind *John 3:8*

- Water *John 7:37–39*

- Seal *Ephesians 1:13*

- Aid *Acts 10:38*

- Dove *Mark 1:10*

SATAN

S atan is the spiritual opponent of God. Originally, Satan was one of God's angels in heaven. Because of pride he became corrupt and challenged God. A war broke out in heaven. Michael the archangel commanded God's army, and Satan was defeated, banished to earth along with those angels in heaven who had sided with him—about a third of all the angels in heaven. This occurred before "the beginning" of creation described in *Genesis 1*. Satan was the "prince of the power of the air." *Ephesians 2:2, Revelation 12:7–9*

The statement in the Bible that the One to defeat Satan would be born of the seed of a woman is the first hint of the virgin birth of Jesus Christ. *Genesis 3:14–15*

Satan was created a perfect being. But later unrighteousness was found in him. *Ezekiel 28:11–19*

Satan fell from perfection when he exerted his will over the will of God, the first time he said, "I will." *Isaiah 14:12–17*

Remember, God created the earth and the Almighty did not create a wasted place. *Isaiah 45:18*

Some believe Satan ruled the earth after his exercise of self-will against God. At Satan's fall from heaven to earth, the earth became formless and void. That catastrophe made the earth formless and void. *Genesis 1:2*

Angels sinned by choosing to follow Satan in the rebellion against God (often referred to as "leaving their first estate"). When they made the choice to follow Satan, they gave up their roles as part of the heavenly family, their "first estate." *Jude 1:6*

Satan is a liar—the father of lies. *John 8:44*

God is true and cannot lie. *Titus 1:2*

Humans are natural and therefore limited; we do not always speak the truth. Sometimes the satanic force is just too powerful for us to overcome. When we refuse to allow God, through Christ and the Holy Spirit, to prevail, we give way to lies, making Satan our father in that moment. *John 8:44*

When the works of the Holy Spirit are attributed to the power of Satan, that is blaspheming the Holy Spirit. *Matthew 12:24*

Those who refuse to believe in God will be damned with Satan. *Revelation 20:14*

Satan has already been defeated. Satan cannot avoid or escape his own doom, nor can his followers theirs. *Revelation 20:7–15*

Satan temps us to keep us from bearing the fruit of the Holy Spirit. *Matthew 16:23, Ephesians 6:11–12*

Believers receive power to resist Satan. *1 Peter 5:8–9*

SIN

*If anyone, then, knows the good they ought
to do and doesn't do it, it is sin for them.*

James 4:17 NIV

Before we talk about what sin is and why it is important to understand, we must consider a couple of facts
about the way humanity views sin. Most people don't
think very much of sin. To some, sin is a religious mirage.
To others, sin is an invention to keep some from doing
what they want. Sin is often denied, with the claim that
"standards change with society," making what was pre-
viously prohibited permissible. Sin is joked about and
laughed at. We laugh when people lie. We joke about
stealing. We brag about adultery.

Others believe sin is a fact, but they do not connect it

with penalty. They believe you can rob the bank without any penalty, if you just don't get caught.

GOD MAKES MUCH OF SIN!

The person who sins will die. *Ezekiel 18:20*
The wages of sin is death. *Romans 6:23*
All sins are an abomination to God. *Proverbs 6:16–19*
God hates those who do iniquity. *Psalm 5:5*

WHAT IS SIN?

Sin is a volitional act (done with knowing effort) of disobedience against the revealed will of God. Everyone who practices sin practices lawlessness. Sin is an evil force that we cannot escape in this life on earth, but it can be overcome by the power of God. The dominion sin has over us is according to the delight we have in it.

Theories of sin vary. To some, sin is a weakness of the flesh, a human frailty. To others, sin is the absence of good. To the scholar, it is ignorance. To the evolutionist, it is the nature of the beast. Recently, sin is seen as a disease to be treated by science; man is not a sinner, he is sick. Sin is also viewed as a form of selfishness.

But God hates sin and declares that sin is

- Lawlessness *1 John 3:4*

- Falling short of the glory of God *Romans 3:23*

- Revolting against God *Isaiah 1:2*

- Unbelief, which makes God a liar *1 John 5:10*

- Going your own way, planning your life according to your own will without seeking the will of God *Isaiah 53:6*

- Unrighteousness *1 John 5:17*

THE CONSEQUENCE OF SIN

There is not a sin that does not carry the death penalty. The consequence of sin is that life ends.
Genesis 3:16–17, Romans 6:23

Sin is a folly to deceive you!
Sin is a force to destroy you!
Sin is a fact that condemns you!

THE ORIGIN OF SIN

The question has often been pondered: Can a good God create sin? Or, if God created everything, does God's creative work include sin? The Bible does not confirm Satan was the originator of sin, as is often assumed, but it does reveal sin in the heart of Satan before God created humanity. The origin of sin is one of the mysteries of the Bible. Human beings will never understand everything, because some secret things belong to the Lord our God. Sin's origin is one of the secret things. *Deuteronomy 29:29*

What the Bible Confirms About Sin

Sin was first noted in the heart of Satan. He wanted to be God. *Revelation 12:19*

Sin entered the world through one man—the first human—Adam. *Romans 5:12*

From Adam, all humans derived their being, and therefore, all partake of this first man's sin and its consequences. *Acts 17:26*

The whole human race comes from Adam. He was the beginning of all humans: spiritually, morally, and physically. Adam was the fountainhead of humanity and man's sole representative before God. He did not act as a single person when he fell. He sinned for all.

Both sin and death came by the transgression of Adam. Adam died—was separated from God—when he sinned. *Genesis 2:17*

Sin caused death to come upon the human race. That

penalty was assessed on Adam and is passed to all his progeny, like spiritual DNA. Death does not come to us because of personal sin as it did in the case of Adam; because of the sin of Adam, all are judged sinners already. We will die because we are sentenced to death, separation from God, because of the sin of the first human if we are not born again. *John 3:3, 3:18*

All humans are born with a sinful nature. *Psalm 51:5*

Sin did not begin with breaking the Law of Moses. The penalty came before the Law of Moses. *Romans 5:13*

THE RESULT OF SIN

Death was passed upon all men because of the sin of Adam. *Romans 5:12*

We sin by choice because we are sinners by nature. *Psalm 51:5*

The wages of sin is death. *Romans 6:23, Ephesians 2:1*

Death does not annihilate; it separates. *Isaiah 59:1–2*

As a result of man's sin, there are three deaths: spiritual, physical, and eternal.

Spiritual Death

Sin separates us from God. *2 Thessalonians 1:9.* Sin drove man from the Garden of Eden. It separated humans from

God spiritually. Where there is sin, there is no contact between that person and God. Sin creates a wall between us. There is no intercourse between God and humanity.

There is only one way back to God. *1 John 1:9*. Admitting our sin to God causes the wall to disappear. Notice that if we do one thing, God does four things:

- God is faithful to us.

- God is just to us.

- God forgives us our sins.

- God cleanses us from all unrighteousness.

Once we confess our sin, we are to forsake sin. We must turn our back on sin; we must not do it anymore; we must not keep practicing it.
Isaiah 55:7, John 5:14, Romans 6:1–2

We pour water on the flaming power of God when we fail to confess our sin. We keep the Holy Spirit from working by not confessing our sin. *Psalm 66:18, Hebrews 6:4–6*

Physical Death

All humans—the good and the bad, the young and the old—die physically. Death is universal. But humanity did not suffer physical death until the first human sinned.

Humanity will continue to die until Jesus Christ destroys death, Christ's last enemy. *1 Corinthians 15:26*

Sin is like a stinger that numbs its victims to a spiritual death. *1 Corinthians 15:54–57*

Eternal Death

The person who dies in sin will die—be eternally separated from God—his or her soul to pass beyond the portal of Hades. *Revelation 20:14-15*

That person is lost and lost forever. *Luke 16:19–31*. The story of Lazarus and the rich man illustrates this. The lost will continue to exist, but are without hope, eternally separated from God.

WE ARE ALL SINNERS

It is a fact that we are sinners, because we fall short of the glory of God. *Romans 3:23*

We must know this and confess our sin to be saved. *1 John 1:9*

Sin is transgressing the laws of God. *1 John 3:4*

The spirit nature of Satan working in us causes us to sin. *1 John 3:8, Romans 8:5–8*

Whosoever commits unrepentant sin breaks the law and incurs the death penalty. *Romans 6:23, James 1:15*

Sin is a real force that can dominate and enslave us. *Romans 6:15–23*

Sin is unbelief; it is calling God a liar. *1 John 5:10*

Sin is disobedience. *1 John 5:17*

Sin is active rebellion against God. *1 Samuel 15:23*

Sin is passive rebellion against God, lack of appreciation of God. *Isaiah 1:2*

God said, "All have sinned one way or another, either by commission or omission, by thought, word, or deed." There are no degrees of penalty when we sin. Unless we turn to Jesus, we have no hope for eternal life. We are already condemned to death. Unless we turn to Jesus, we will be eternally separated from God. Having the knowledge of separation without taking action to be born again is itself sin.

God's Remedy for Sin

When you become ill, you go see a doctor who has some expertise concerning your complaint and can remedy the physical problem. Sin is a spiritual illness that all of us are born with. Our general practitioners are preachers, who continually direct us to God through Jesus Christ, God's remedy for sin. But most people are not willing to accept salvation and instead try to deal with sin by human means.

Understanding God's remedy for sin:

- Righteousness of God *2 Corinthians 5:21*

- Regeneration *Titus 3:5*

Jesus redeemed all people by dying in their place. *1 Peter 2:24*

Humanity needs to be justified by faith in Jesus Christ; no one is justified by works of law, or the good that we do. *Galatians 2:16*

Salvation is not brought about by cleaning up our old selves. We must be made anew in Christ. The spirit and nature of God is in the renewed person. *Ephesians 4:24.* If we are new people, our whole lives will flow in a different direction. Our new life, our new nature will manifest righteousness and holiness.

Salvation comes by the grace of God, which means it is a gift of God. *Ephesians 2:8–9*

The gift is only given to those who have a clean heart. *Psalm 24:3–5*

A clean heart comes from confessing sin. When we confess our sin, God will cleanse our hearts and fill us as new vessels with righteousness. *1 John 1:9*

HUMAN EFFORTS TO REMEDY SIN

Instead of admitting our sin to God and asking forgiveness based on the sacrifice of Jesus, we strive to handle our shortcomings in the following ways:

- With self-righteousness from deeds
  Isaiah 64:6, Proverbs 20:6

- Striving to reform our life *Proverbs 16:2*

- Turning over a new leaf
  Ecclesiastes 1:16–17, Luke 11:24–26

- Justifying our conduct *Matthew 19:16–30, Romans 12:3*

- Cleaning up our act *Proverbs 20:9*

- Doing good works *Galatians 2:16, Ephesians 2:8–9*

Sin is an evil force that can be overcome by God. God's remedy for sin was to substitute Jesus Christ, who had no sin, for us. When Jesus went to the cross, He did not have any of His own sins to pay for, so He died for our sins instead. He is the sole remedy for our sins, but only if we put faith in Christ as our personal Savior. Christ alone bore our sins, and is therefore the only source of our spiritual redemption.

REPENTANCE

The Lord is not slow in keeping his promise,
as some understand slowness. Instead he
is patient with you, not wanting anyone to
perish, but everyone to come to repentance.

2 Peter 3:9 NIV

Those who reject and forsake sin will find compassion. God desires truth and commands all, everywhere, to repent. *Proverbs 28:13, Acts 17:30*

Repentance toward God shows faith in the Gospel of Jesus Christ that Christ died for our sins, was buried, and rose from the dead. *1 Corinthians 15:1–4.* Repentance is an inward change produced by the power of Holy Spirit.

The sinner must repent before receiving salvation by

grace through faith. The sinner repents before knowing the meaning of repentance. *Ephesians 2:8–9*

Christians must practice repentance to enjoy unbroken fellowship with God. *Acts 10:43, 1 John 1:5–10*

Repentance is a gift from God. The kindness of God leads to repentance. The kindness of God is not merited. We do not deserve it. *Act 5:31, Romans 2:4*

REPENTANCE DEFINED

Repentance is godly sorrow, a guilty feeling that leads to Christ. *2 Corinthians 7:9–10*

Repentance is without regret because it leads to salvation. Repentance is not penance. If we could be saved by penance, then salvation would not be a gift and we would not be saved by grace through faith in Jesus Christ. Penance is to render payment for one's sin. It is an act or deed. The price for sin—prior, present, and future—was paid by Christ. God calls no one to penance.

Jesus did not say we should repent and do penance! He said we should repent and believe in the Gospel and receive the gift of salvation. *Mark 1:15*

Peter did not say we should do penance and be baptized! He said we should repent and be baptized. *Acts 2:38*

Paul did not say that God commanded everyone to do penance! He said that God commanded all to repent. *Acts 17:30*

Repentance is not reformation. *Matthew 12:43–45*. Reformation is a change brought on by efforts of an individual—not by God's Spirit or God's Word. Reformation is turning over a new leaf or making restitution.

Repentance is a change that involves three elements:

- Intellect—a change of mind

- Emotion—a change of heart

- Volition—a change of will

An illustration is the prodigal son. *Luke 15:11–32*

- "He came to his senses"—intellectual *Luke 15:17*

- "I have sinned"—emotional *Luke 15:21*

- "I will give up and go home"—volitional *Luke 15:18*

No one ever repents until he or she wants to. In godly repentance, a person's actions change. If there is no change in action, there is no repentance.

REPENTANCE PREACHED

Repentance was proclaimed in the Old Testament. It is one of the foundational principles of Christianity. Repentance was proclaimed before Christ's birth. Christ preached it. Peter did at Pentecost. Repentance is taught in the Epistles. It is also taught in the book of Revelation.

John the Baptist preached a baptism of repentance. *Luke 3:3*

Jesus preached: "Repent and believe in the Gospel." *Mark 1:14–15*

Peter preached repentance at Pentecost. *Acts 2:38*

Paul preached that everyone should repent. He gave this message on Mars Hill to the intellectuals of Athens. *Acts 17:32–33*

REPENTANCE REPEATED

Christians backslide. This means we repent and then sometimes make huge mistakes or commit gross sins.

Simon Peter backslid. *Matthew 26:69–75*. He denied any knowledge of Christ, but he repented and was restored to fellowship with Christ. *John 21:3–17*

King David sinned, committed adultery, tried to cover up the act, and committed murder. *2 Samuel 11:1–27*. He repented and was restored to fellowship with the Lord. *Psalm 51:1–19, 2 Samuel 12:13*

These biblical examples show us that a Christian who backslides can repent and be restored to fellowship with God.

Hebrews 6:4–6 does not refer to Christians who backslide, but to those who were once enlightened and professed faith but do not possess eternal life because they never became Christians.

THE CHURCH

*Keep watch over yourselves and all the
flock of which the Holy Spirit has made you
overseers. Be shepherds of the church of
God, which he bought with his own blood.*

Acts 20:28 NIV

The Church is the earth-wide congregation, or community, of those who share belief in Jesus Christ. "The Church" also refers to the all-inclusive Church in earth and heaven.

THE CHURCH OF JESUS CHRIST

The Church is not an actual building, although it is compared to a building. *Ephesians 2:19–22*

Jesus is the foundation and head of the Church. Jesus is the foundation the Church is built upon. Belief in Jesus Christ is the true foundation of Christianity. Jesus is the head of the all-inclusive Church on earth and in heaven. *Ephesians 2:20*

Jesus Christ tells His closest followers that the Church will be based on the truth that Jesus is the Son of the Living God. *Matthew 16:13–18*

When Jesus asked the disciples, "Who do you think I am?" and Peter answered, "The Son of the living God" (*Matthew 16:16*), the source and meaning of Peter's answer was the Holy Spirit. Peter's human knowledge and experience did not reveal it. No mortal being revealed the information. Divine revelations are always by the Holy Spirit, not by human thinking or wisdom.

Christ referred to Simon as Peter (Greek, *petros*, a rock). *Matthew 16:18*. *Petros* means a physical rock, but the Church is not built on Peter, it is built on a large, immovable rock (Greek, *petras*), who is Jesus Christ. Christ is the only foundation of the Church.

Jesus is the head of the Church. *Colossians 1:18*

Jesus is its cornerstone. *1 Peter 2:6–7*

Jesus Christ is the final and absolute authority. He has never delegated the authority to anyone, not to pope, bishop, pastor, deacon, nor the majority of the congregation that make up a church. *Ephesians 1:21–23*

BELIEVERS ARE THE BUILDING STONES OF THE CHURCH

The Church is built of believers. *Peter 2:5*

Believers are built into the structure of the Church. *Ephesians 2:21*. The Church continually increases in size through new converts.

There is no difference between the Church and "the body of Christ" in the Bible. The Church is referred to as the body of Christ in numerous passages of the Bible. *Ephesians 1:22–23, Colossians 1:24, 1 Corinthians 12:27.*

Born-again, blood-washed, Spirit-baptized believers form the Church. The only way to become a Church member is to be spiritually reborn, baptized into it by the Holy Spirit. You cannot join this Church any other way. *Ephesians 4:6, 2 Thessalonians 2:13–15*

THE CHURCH AS THE BODY OF CHRIST

The Bible compares the Church to the human body. *1 Corinthians 12:1–31*. All believers in Christ are a part of the same body. Just as the human body has many parts working together to make the body function, the congregation of Christ has many different types of persons, all functioning to make the Church the spiritual body of Christ. *1 Corinthians 12:12*

All Christians make up the body of Christ but differ as to their functions. *1 Corinthians 12:27–31*

The members are given spiritual gifts according to the will of the Holy Spirit. *1 Corinthians 12:1–11*

The body of Christ, like the human body, has many members with different operations, but all are related and coordinated under one head, Jesus Christ. *1 Corinthians 12:12*

The Church is many members functioning as one in the will of God. *1 Corinthians 12:14–18*

The weakest member is necessary for the proper function of the body. *1 Corinthians 12:22–23*

If one member suffers, the whole body suffers. *1 Corinthians 12:26*

If one member is honored, all are honored. *1 Corinthians 12:26*

Members are to minister in love and are to desire the greater spiritual gift. *1 Corinthians 12:31*

The Holy Spirit is the agent who brings members into the body of Christ. *Romans 8:9, Titus 3:5-6*

No matter our background or nationality, what we've done, or where we've been, we all join the congregation (body) the same way, by

- Being baptized by the Spirit of God
  1 Corinthians 12:13

- Living godly consecrated lives *1 Corinthians 6:16-18*

- Cooperating and avoiding confusion or strife
  1 Corinthians 12:15–17

- Recognizing that each member needs the other
  members to keep the Church functioning
  1 Corinthians 12:21

- Seeking to please God in whatever part we play
  1 Corinthians 12:22–25

- Relating to all members of the Church
  sympathetically *1 Corinthians 12:24–26*

- Loving the gifts given to each member (not being
  jealous) *1 Corinthians 12:29–31*

- Being sympathetic (not apathetic) to members'
  faults *Galatians 6:1, 1 Corinthians 13:4–7*

Jesus Christ entrusted the Church (believers) to continue proclaiming the Gospel. We are to proclaim it wherever we go, throughout the whole world (the present social order). *Matthew 28:19, Acts 10:34*

THE CHURCH IS REFERRED TO AS THE BRIDE OF CHRIST

The Church is also compared to a bride. (The apostle Paul alludes to the customs of special care of virgins. Paul was protective of his converts; he wanted to present his converts to Christ just as a chosen virgin was presented to her husband. Concerning this verse, some teach that the Church is compared to a virgin. But Paul states that the Church is the bride of Christ. The verse is not proof that a virgin is the symbol of the Church.) *2 Corinthians 11:2*

These verses comparing the Church to a bride show Christ's intense love for the Church and total commitment to the Church. *Ephesians 5:28–31*

- Those in the Church are to be educated. The teaching, caring, and training are to make the body of Christ glorious. *Ephesians 5:26–28*

- The Church is to be kept pure. Paul wanted his converts to remain pure, meaning not affected by false doctrine. *2 Corinthians 11:2*

- The Church is set apart from the world. Christ is one with his Church in spirit. *Ephesians 5:25–27*

THE CHURCH IS A MYSTERY

The Bible calls the Church a mystery. *Ephesians 3:3–10*

The mystery of the congregation was not understood by the Old Testament prophets. The Old Testament prophets were Hebrews—Jewish. In the Church, non-Jews (Gentiles) and Jews who believed in Jesus Christ came together. The promises of God in the Old Testament part of the Bible were made to Jewish people, but non-Jews also enjoyed the benefits of those promises when God made them a reality. In the Church, God made Jews and non-Jews one group, members of one new body. *Acts 10:34–35, Galatians 3:26–28*

THE CHURCH ORGANIZATION

The Church is more than a religious organization. It is an organism, with Christ the living head. It is alive. Christ lives through each member of the Church.
2 Corinthians 3:3, 1 John 3:24, Galatians 2:20

The majority of the Bible's references to Church organization refer to the local Church.
Acts 9:31, Hebrews 13:17, Titus 1:4–5

Officers in the Church. *Ephesians 4:11–12*

- Apostles refer to the original twelve disciples. There are no apostles today.

- Prophets are those who sense what to expect in the future. The last prophet, John, wrote the book of Revelation.

- Evangelists are missionaries of the Gospel, proclaimers of the message of Jesus Christ.

- Pastors are ministers to the Church. They pass on spiritual messages in the context of the Church.

- Teachers communicate spiritual truth and provide instruction in the Gospel.

- Deacons are ordained to assist the pastor by ministering to the Church members. Note that they are never called a board in the Scriptures. They are to serve the believers, not to run the Church. *1 Timothy 3:8–13, Acts 6:1–7*

Local Church business is conducted through membership meetings, which are like local business meetings. *Acts 1:15–26*

Membership records are information about the Church. On the day of Pentecost, Peter was the pastor and records were that three thousand believers were added to the Church. *Acts 2:41*

Another five thousand believers were added on another occasion. *Acts 4:4.*

CHURCH DISCIPLINE OF BELIEVERS

Discipline is a necessary function of the local church. Although difficult, it is very important. The church has a responsibility to address sin in the membership so that it does not spread throughout the congregation. *1 Corinthians 5:6–7.* The motive for corrective action always is love, not punishment or judgment. *Galatians 6:1*

The goal is to restore the church through a three-step approach to resolving any conflict in the church. *Matthew 18:15–17*

These are the three steps:

- Members should settle all personal differences by themselves. The member who has been sinned against should take the initiative for reconciliation, not revenge.

- Members should have their personal efforts confirmed by two or three witnesses if the sinner does not listen and does not repent.

- Members should take a stubborn and unforgiving brother before the church. If he refuses all means of reconciliation, he should be excommunicated. If he repents, the church's attitude should be one of forgiveness and love.

THE WORSHIP OF GOD BY THE CHURCH

To worship is to bow down to God, to humbly pay divine honor to him. The three essentials of worship are faith, spirit, and truth:

- Faith: The people believed, then bowed low and worshipped. *Exodus 4:31*

- Spirit: Those who worship him must worship in spirit. *John 4:23–24*

    Spirit worship is directed by the Holy Spirit in you. *Philemon 3:3*

- Truth: Jesus Christ is truth. *John 14:6*

Believers must worship God in spirit and truth. *John 4:24*

THE WORK OF THE CHURCH

The main focus of the Church is to share its faith with the lost, going everywhere and sharing the Gospel. *Matthew 28:16–20*

The need of the Church to work is great. *John 4:35, Matthew 9:35–38*

The time is now for the Church to work. *2 Corinthians 6:2*

The Church is to work until Jesus returns. *Philippians 1:16*

When Jesus comes, He will judge the work of individuals in the Church. *2 Corinthians 5:10*

The Church will receive a reward for its works. *1 Corinthians 3:9–15*

The Church is to wage spiritual warfare. *Ephesians 6:10–18*

Believers are to put on the full armor of a heavily armed soldier. *Ephesians 6:13–17*

- We are given the ability to stand against all enemies. *Ephesians 6:11–14*

- We are given the ability to withstand all attacks. *Ephesians 6:13*

- We are given the ability to extinguish every fiery dart of Satan's. *Ephesians 6:16*

The Church is to run a race. *Hebrews 12:1–2*
To run effectively, we must

- Lay aside whatever hinders progress, such as arrogance or conceit. *Hebrews 12:1*

- Lay aside any sin a person has been addicted to. *Hebrews 12:1*

- Exercise patience—fight conflict and contentions. *Philippians 2:1–4*

The Church is to work in love. *Ephesians 4:2–3*
We believers work along with God. We are God's farm; we produce Christians. We are farming people, harvesting souls.

THE POWER OF THE CHURCH

On the day of Pentecost the Church received power. *Acts 1:1–47*

The 120 believers in the upper room were the same as believers are today, indwelt with the Holy Spirit for carrying out the works of Christ. Some received power for special service, miracle-working power, sin-converting power, the power necessary to evangelize the world. All received the power to witness. *Acts 2:32*

The real power of the Church is not found in modern buildings or unique methods of preaching and teaching. The Gospel is the same no matter how it is told. Let Christ become commander of your life. Let God's will, not yours, be done. *Hebrews 13:20-21, James 1:5-6*

The real power of the Church has nothing to do with Church wealth or how it is used. The message is the same, and the power to witness is the same, with or without wealth, spent wisely or not.

1 Timothy 6:3–10, 1 Thessalonians 1:1–10

The real power of the Church has nothing to do with popularity or prominence. Laodicea was the first bragging church; unfortunately, it was not the last.

Revelation 3:14–22

It was indifferent and careless. *3:15*

It was proud and self-satisfied. *3:17*

It was ignorant of its true state. *3:17*

It felt rich. *3:17*

It increased in material things, rather than godly things. *3:17*

What God said about the church of Laodicea applies to many churches today:

Laodicea's members said they were rich. God said they were poor. *3:17*

They said they were wealthy. God said they were wretched. *3:17*

They said they did not need anything. God said they needed everything. *3:18*

They said they were busy in church. God said they were miserable. *3:1–2*

They said they had a vision. God said they were blind. *3:17*

They said they had fine clothes. God said they were naked. *3:17*

They said they were satisfied. God said they made Him sick. *3:16*

A HOLY SPIRIT–EMPOWERED CHURCH

Evangelizes—shares its faith with others and teaches the Word of God, the Bible. Souls are saved. *Acts 2:36–41*

Evangelism is full proof of ministry. The Spirit-filled believer shares Bible truth. The Holy Spirit convicts the listeners of their sins and leads them to repentance. The Holy Spirit is grieved when a church is not involved in saving lost souls. Such a church is devoid of power because the only reason to have power is to win souls.

Reproduces. Romans 10:10–17

Evangelism causes the Church to grow, as new souls are born again and become part of the family of God.

Sees change in people, places, and circumstances.

- People—Look at the effect of Peter's sermon. *Acts 2:37–41*

- Places—Because of preaching, the city of Jerusalem changed. *Acts 5:28*

- Circumstances—such as the power to change through prayer and fasting. *Matthew 17:20–21*

Turns the world upside down. *Acts 17:6*

Social systems and priorities have changed because of Spirit-filled churches.

The same power that filled the upper room on Pentecost is with the believer today. That power is the Holy Spirit whose entry into the world was dramatic. That power is no less today.

THE FUTURE OF THE CHURCH

The true Church of Jesus Christ has a glorious, victorious future. It cannot and will not fail. The gates of Hades shall not overpower it. *Matthew 16:18*

Note that those gates did prevail against the Old Testament saints, for they all went down to paradise, a compartment of Hades, and were held captive against their will by Satan. *Hebrews 2:14–15*

Christ conquered hell and liberated the righteous souls. Saints of this age now go to heaven at death instead of to Hades. *Mark 16:15–16, Romans 10:9*

The Future of the Church in the World

The Church will be victorious through Jesus. The Church cannot fail because the Holy Spirit is its power. The Word of God—the Bible—is its guide.
2 Timothy 3:15–17, Romans 15:4

The Future of the Church in the "Air"

The Church will experience the rapture—believers will meet our Lord Jesus in the heavens, in his resurrected body. *1 Thessalonians 4:17, 1 John 3:2*

The Future of the Church in the Kingdom

The twelve apostles will sit on thrones and judge the twelve tribes of Israel. *Matthew 19:28*

All other believers will sit on the throne with Jesus Christ. *Revelation 3:21*

Believers will reign with Jesus as kings and priests for one thousand years. *Revelation 20:4–6*

The Future of the Church in Eternity

After the thousand-year reign of Jesus, there will be a new heaven and a new earth. *Revelation 21:1.* This newness is not created out of nothing as God did in the Genesis creation, but rather, it represents a transformed earth.

This third and eternal state will be perfect, bringing God's creation back to its original state. *Genesis 1:1*

God's earthly people will inherit the new earth forever, as God promised to give Abraham, Isaac, and Jacob and their descendants a new land. *Genesis 17:8, 26:3–5, 27:28–29; Revelation 21:1–7*

The body of believers—those believing in Jesus Christ as their Savior—are referred to as the Church and will remain in God's presence forever. Whether Jesus is in the new heaven or the new earth, believers will be with him to see his face, to worship him, and to serve him. *1 John 3:2, Revelation 22:4*

God will bestow eternal grace upon believers. *Ephesians 2:6–7*

Even in our perfect bodies, it will take time without end, eternity, for us to comprehend the greatness of God's grace.

BAPTISM AND COMMUNION
(THE LORD'S SUPPER)

The Church is the community we are baptized into. Water baptism is the outward manifestation that we have repented and are born again. It does not change anyone physically nor does it put away the filth of the flesh. Once we are baptized, we should become a functioning part of the body. We should fight against evil entering into the body, not bring evil into the body.

Baptism brings us into the body of Christ. *1 Corinthians 12:13*. What is called "one baptism" is the only way anyone can become part of body.

The Holy Spirit is the agent to baptize us into Christ.

Ephesians 4:5. The best time for baptism is at repentance and the new birth.

The minister of the local church is the principal agent to baptize. *Matthew 28:19, Acts 6:15, Ephesians 4:11.* Baptism is linked to fellowship with other believers and to mutual responsibility. Therefore baptism has become a function of the local church.

Spirit Baptism

Spirit baptism is the endowment by the Holy Spirit with the power to serve. *John 7:37–39*

Anyone will receive Spirit baptism who

- Thirsts, has a craving and passion for complete union with God and the fullness of God's Spirit. *John 7:37*

- Completely surrenders his or her life to do the will of God as he or she receives light or knowledge. *John 1:17, Acts 2:38, Acts 10:44–47*

- Receives the gifts, fruits, and operation of the Holy Spirit wholeheartedly. *John 7:39*

- Believes the whole Gospel. *John 7:38*

Jesus Christ is the agent to baptize us in the Holy Spirit. *Matthew 3:11*

Spirit baptism can occur before or after water baptism. *Acts 10:44*

CHURCH ORDINANCES

Ordinances are the rules and requirements of the Church. There are only two:

- **Baptism.**

Baptism identifies believers with the risen Savior. Baptism does not save. It is an outward manifestation of belief in the death, burial, and resurrection of Jesus Christ. It is faith that saves. *Matthew 3:13–15, Ephesians 2:8*

- **The Lord's Supper.**

Also called "Communion" or "the bread and wine" or "Eucharist" or "Sacrament," the Lord's Supper is observed by believers to proclaim the death of the Lord Jesus until He returns. There is no saving power in the Lord's Supper; it is a memorial. The bread is symbolic of the body of Jesus. The wine is symbolic of Jesus' shed blood. It is a reminder of Christ's suffering for the remission of our sins. *1 Corinthians 10:16, 11:26*

DEATH

C hrist's resurrection gave believers eternal life. Believers will not stay dead, but will live again in imperishable glorified bodies. *1 Corinthians 15:42–44*

These spirit bodies will be as real as can be, but of a higher substance than our natural bodies. We don't know what our new bodies will be like, but we do know that our bodies will be like Jesus' resurrected body. We will be recognized as the same persons we were on earth—we will have the same color, features, and characteristics. Resurrected bodies will be flesh and bone, but not flesh and blood. *Luke 24:39, Philemon 3:21*

At the rapture, believers will meet the Lord Jesus in the heavens, in His resurrected body. *1 John 3:2*

Believers Will Not Come into Judgment for Sin

All believers have eternal life. *John 5:24*

The sins of the believers have already been judged on the cross. Those who have faith in Jesus were judged in Christ on the cross, and Jesus Christ paid the penalty for their sin. Their salvation is present (now). They are already acquitted of sin in God's eyes because Jesus Christ paid for their sins. When a person is born again, all prior sins are washed away. The person comes as a newborn baby with no contamination. *John 3:18, 1 Timothy 2:6*

Every believer has passed "out of death into life." *1 John 3:14*

Because Jesus Christ paid the penalty for the believer's sin, that person is no longer identified with wrongdoing. The believer is separated from sin forever in God's eyes, as far as the east is separated from the west. *Psalm 103:12*

The believer's sins are wiped out, and God will not remember the believer's sins. *Isaiah 43:25*

Jesus Christ suffered for our sins—"The just for the unjust"—that we might be saved and never come into judgment as sinners. *1 Peter 3:18*

God sent Jesus and made Him to be sin on our behalf. *2 Corinthians 5:21*

The believer will not face this first judgment because the believer's sins have been purified. *Hebrews 1:3*

Judgment of the Believer's Self

The judgment of the believer's self is intended by God to promote the believer to judge themself, to examine the good and bad in their life. The believer will confess the bad and forsake the bad. We confess our sin, ask for forgiveness, and put it away. *Isaiah 55:7*

As we anticipate this judgment, we must judge ourselves, now. *1 Corinthians 11:31–32*

For this self-judgment, the believer must

- Renounce the self. *Matthew 16:24*. We must see the self as God sees us: dirty, unclean, and unworthy. This is replacing self-life with Christ-life. Christ is the believer's life.

- Deny the self. *Romans 12:2*. This is more than self-denial, which is denying ourselves of the gratification of the flesh. Self-denial is treating the symptom, not the cause. To deny the self is to attack the cause by yielding to Jesus Christ. *Mark 8:34–38*. To deny the self is to take up our cross and follow Jesus—habitually, daily, and willingly.

- Lose the self-life (*Galatians 2:20*) and find the Christ-life.

- Cease being self-conscious, but become Christ-conscious. *Philippians 2:2–5*

- Relinquish self-control and become Christ-controlled. *Romans 8:5*

- Forgo self-esteem and practice esteeming others better or higher than the self. *Philippians 2:3.* Some religions teach that high self-esteem is important, but Christian self-esteem is rooted in knowing our value to God.

The believer is to judge the self or be judged by the Lord Jesus Christ and be disciplined. We avoid chastening by judging ourselves. If we refuse to judge ourselves, God judges by chastening, so we will not be condemned. We reap what we sow if we do not self-judge. *1 Corinthians 11:31–37*

JUDGMENT OF BELIEVER'S WORKS

The believer's earthly deeds or works will be judged at the judgment seat of Christ. *2 Corinthians 5:10*

Only believers will appear at the judgment seat of Christ. At judgment, believers will receive rewards or suffer the loss of potential rewards based upon what we did while living the life of a born-again believer. *1 Corinthians 3:11–15*

Believers' works will be judged, but not their sins because all believers' sins were judged in Christ on Calvary. *Romans 8:1*

This judgment of works will take place in the air following the first resurrection. Those who died believing in Christ will rise first, before those alive at the coming of the Lord. *1 Thessalonians 4:14–18*

Note: There will be a thousand years between the resurrection of those who believed in Jesus and those who died without faith in Christ. The second judgment will be the Great White Throne Judgment, where only the unsaved will appear at the judgment seat of Christ. *Romans 14:10–13*

There are three primary beliefs regarding the return of Christ to rule on earth for a period of time, possibly a thousand years. *Revelation 20*

The postmillennialist view accepts that Christ will return to earth to rule only after His kingdom has been established on earth by Christians.

The premillennialists believe that Christ will return before the thousand-year period to judge unbelievers, and that He will reign bodily on the earth during the millennium.

Amillennialists reject the interpretation of this passage as a physical thousand-year reign of Christ on earth.

All believers will give an account of their life at the judgment and some will be ashamed. *1 John 2:28*

Some will suffer loss, but not loss of salvation. Theirs will be a loss of rewards. *1 Corinthians 3:11–15*

We will receive rewards according to our labor. *1 Corinthians 3:8*

Believers will be judged concerning

- Doctrine *Romans 2:14–16*

- Conduct toward others *Romans 14*

- Carnal traits *Colossians 3:1–16, Romans 1:25*

- Words *Matthew 12:32, 35–37*

- Relationships with others, including slander, quarrels, idle words, folly, dishonesty, broken promises, and wrong dealing *1 Corinthians 6:9–11, Romans 1:29–32, Galatians 5:19–21*

- Relationship with the self (*Romans 12:3, Proverbs 26:12*), including neglected opportunity (*Luke 6:46*), wasted talents (*Matthew 25:14–30*), loose living (*Hebrews 10:26–31*), and lack of spirituality (*John 12:43, 2 Timothy 3:1–9*)

- Relationship with God, including refusal to live according to Christ's example (*2 Timothy 4:3*), yielding to invitations of nonbelievers and being disobedient to God (*Ephesians 5:11*), rejection of God's transformation (*Romans 12*), and failure to cooperate with and yield to the Holy Spirit (*Ephesians 4:1–6*)

JUDGMENT OF THE NATIONS AND THE WICKED

For we will all stand before the judgment seat of God; for it is written, "As I live, says the Lord, every knee shall bow to me, and every tongue shall confess to God." So then each of us will give an account of himself to God.

Romans 14:10–12 ESV

Five separate judgments are revealed in the Word of God. They differ as to time, place, and purpose, but all have one thing in common: the Lord Jesus Christ is the judge. *John 5:22*

It is essential to understand that these judgments cannot be considered one general judgment. The three judgments relevant to believers are discussed in the previous chapter—the judgments for sin (from which believers are exempt), self, and deeds.

JUDGMENT OF THE NATIONS

Judgment of the nations will come after the tribulations, at the Second Advent when Christ comes to set up His kingdom. *Matthew 25:31–46*

It will not be a judgment of every individual, it is not a judgment of the wicked who have died, but of all the nations involved with Israel. The judgment will take place when the Son of Man comes in glory. *Matthew 25:37*

The purpose is to determine which nations will inherit the earth. The meek shall be given the earth as promised. *Matthew 5:5*

The basis of the judgment is how a nation has dealt with Israel. God will curse or bless accordingly. This is the fulfillment of God's covenant with Abraham. *Genesis 12:1–3*

The judgment will be of existing nations in the earthly kingdom of Christ or God. *Matthew 24–25*

These are facts about the judgment of the nations:

- When: immediately after the tribulation, the Second Advent of Christ *Matthew 24:29–31, 25:31*

- Place: on earth, in and around Jerusalem *Joel 3:1–2*

- How: Christ will exert power *Matthew 25:31*

JUDGMENT OF THE WICKED

The wicked dead are to be judged at the Great White Throne Judgment. The Judge will again be the Lord Jesus Christ. God will judge by His Son Jesus Christ. God will decree; the Son—Jesus—will execute. *Revelation 20:11–15*

Only the wicked dead will be judged. *Revelation 20:5.* (The believers will have been resurrected a thousand years earlier and their works judged then. See page 74.) This will include all the wicked dead, from Adam to the end of the millennium.

It will be a literal, visible, personal trial, similar to trials on earth. *Revelation 20:6, 21:8*

The wicked dead will seek a hiding place. They will seek to escape from the face of the Lord Christ, but there will be no escape. *Romans 1:18*

Great and small will stand before the throne, but greatness will have no impact because no one has done good. *Romans 3:12*

The books that will be opened as the basis of judgment (*Revelation 20:12*) when the dead will be judged according to their deeds are

- Law of Consciences, Character, and Conduct— based on the light received. *Romans 2:12*

- Law of Memory—The rich man lost his opportunity to do the will of God. *Luke 16:25*

- Law of Character—feelings. *Ephesians 4:19*

- Law of Moses and Gospel—based on knowledge of these. *Romans 2:16*

- Record of personal acts. *Luke 12:2–9*

- The book of life—names are blotted out. *Revelation 22:19*. Although there are no believers in this judgment, the book of life (*Romans 1:18–20*) is referenced because at this judgment, the wicked will be shown that God, with great mercy, provided a place for them in the book of life, but they did not receive it. *John 12:48*

In summary, there will be no acquittals, no high court to which the lost may appeal. The lost are sentenced to hell, where God's love does not extend. The length of the sentence is eternity.

SALVATION VS. REWARDS

*Whatever you do, work at it with all your
heart, as working for the Lord, not for human
masters, since you know that you will receive
an inheritance from the Lord as a reward. It
is the Lord Christ you are serving.*

Colossians 3:23–24 NIV

We are sometimes confused as to the meaning of
the words "salvation" and "rewards." There is a big difference between the doctrine of salvation for the lost
and rewards for the saved.

DOCTRINE OF SALVATION FOR THE LOST

The simplest statement of how we are resurrected spiritually from death because of our sins is that we are saved by the grace of God. Salvation is a gift from God. We do no labor for it. We do not earn salvation. *Ephesians 2:8–10*

We are saved through our belief, through faith, in the life, death, and resurrection of Jesus Christ. *John 3:16*

DOCTRINE OF REWARDS FOR BELIEVERS

Rewards are according to the works of the believer. *1 Corinthians 3:8–15*

All believers will be rewarded according to their own labor or works. Rewards are not given according to the success of labor but according to the motives and faithfulness of service. *1 Corinthians 3:8*

CROWNS OR WREATHS

Rewards are called crowns or wreaths. *James 1:12*

How do we earn the crown of life, which is sometimes referred to as the lover's crown? The crown of life is given to the one who endures trials and temptations. *Luke 6:22*

The believer finds strength to endure through the love of God. *Romans 5:3–5*

Without the love of God in the heart of the believer, trials can cause one to be bitter or critical and lose the crown of life. *Hebrews 12:7*

The crown of life will be given to those who are faithful until death. To receive this crown the believer must love the Lord more than their own life. The reward will be given to those who live for Christ, not the self, and endure trials in the power of the love of God. *Revelation 2:10*

God can help us withstand any temptation. In order not to yield to temptation, we must depend upon our faith and union with God. This is what will determine how well we stand and withstand. When we stand alone in certain areas of our lives, we are losing to the enemy, even when we think we are winning. We cannot withstand the enemy without God. *1 Corinthians 10:13*

The wreath in the Greek games is the model for the emblem of winning the spiritual race, the imperishable wreath of believers. *1 Corinthians 9:24–27*

Just as young men in the games had to be Greek, only born-again believers are eligible for spiritual rewards. Just as the participant in the games must deny himself many gratifications of the body, believers must buffet their bodies and make their bodies their slave. Just as participants in the games were disqualified and would not get the prize if they did not follow the rules, believers who do not follow the rules of Christ will be disqualified and will lose the imperishable wreath.

They cannot be spiritual spectators. The New Testament contains the rules for believers who would enter the spiritual race to win the imperishable wreath. They must

- Deny the self of anything that holds them back. *Hebrews 12:1*

- Keep their eyes fixed on Jesus. *Hebrews 12:2*

- Find strength in the Lord. *Ephesians 6:10–18*

- Place all upon the altar of the Lord. *Romans 12:1*

- Refuse anything that impedes or interferes with their spiritual growth or progress. *Hebrews 11:24–29*

Five things believers must do to win the prize:

- Run the spiritual race all-out. *1 Corinthians 9:24*

- Be temperate in all things. *1 Corinthians 9:27*

- Fight with absolute confidence of winning. *1 Corinthians 9:24*

- Keep the body under subjection. *1 Corinthians 9:25*

- Not let the body control the mind. *1 Corinthians 9:26*

The crown of exultation, which is the soul winner's crown, is for bringing others to the knowledge of Christ. *1 Thessalonians 2:19–20*

A believer's greatest work, and greatest privilege, is to bring others to the knowledge of Christ as their personal Savior. Our degree of joy in heaven will be determined by those we have had a part in bringing to Christ. Every soul winner will shine as the stars forever. *Daniel 12:3*

To bring others to Christ is

- Wise *Proverbs 11:30*

- A work against sin *James 5:20*

- Cause for joy in heaven *Luke 15:10*

Ways believers can bring souls to Christ:

- Allow others to see Christ in them. *2 Corinthians 3:2*

- Trust the Holy Spirit to give power to their spoken Word. *Acts 1:8*

- With tithes and other offerings help others preach Christ. *2 Corinthians 9:6, Philippians 4:14–17*

The crown of righteousness is a gift to be accepted by the believer when they become a Christian. This is made possible by Christ's becoming sin on our behalf. *2 Corinthians 5:21, 2 Timothy 4:5–8*

PRAYER

And pray in the Spirit on all occasions
with all kinds of prayers and requests. With
this in mind, be alert and always keep on
praying for all the saints.

Ephesians 6:18 NIV

Prayer springs from the heart with a need greater than man is able to fulfill. It is man's acknowledgment of a being higher than himself. It is practiced by people of all faiths in some form. It is as instinctive as breathing. Even at this, few people know how to pray, yet many call on God. *Genesis 4:26*

Prayer is a rare privilege because it brings us into close fellowship with God as we admit our need for and show our total dependence upon God.

Two kinds of prayer are reflected in the parable of the Pharisee and the publican. *Luke 18:9–14*

One kind is prayer that reaches God—The publican who came feeling unworthy prayed and did reach God.

The other kind is prayer that does not reach God— The Pharisee brought his self-righteous prayer and did not reach God.

Both went to the same place, at the same time, for the same purpose, to pray. Only one was heard.

God's purpose in answering prayer is to help us and confirm the infinite Fatherhood of God. No good thing will God withhold from us. *Matthew 21:22, Psalm 84:11*

WHAT PRAYER IS

The Lord instructs the believer to ask, seek, and knock because these three words really cover the whole spectrum of prayer. On the surface, the instructions seem simple. Most fail to recognize the immensity of the instructions. *Matthew 7:7–11*

Asking and Receiving

Regarding a need, whether material or spiritual, when you know the will of God and know the Almighty hears you in whatever you ask, you can ask and receive.

This is prayer according to the revealed Word of God. *1 John 5:14–15*

Seeking and Finding

When the will of God is not known concerning a material or spiritual need, you are to seek God's will, in prayer, concerning the need until you find what God's will is. This is a prayer for knowledge of the unrevealed will of God, concerning a specific need. *Jeremiah 29:12–13, Colossians 3:1*

Until you know if your need (perhaps a job or blessing) is in God's will, do not ask, or ask conditionally, for example, "Here is my request, Lord, but let Your will be done." In determining if your need is within the will of God or not, look to Scripture for help.

Knocking and Opening

When you know the will of God but find a closed door—your prayer was not received—you are to knock until the door is opened. This is tenacious prayer, a no-quitting prayer, prayer with mountain-moving faith, miracle-working prayer. Keep praying until the impossible becomes possible. *Matthew 7:7–8, 17:14–21*

Asking, seeking, and knocking are possible only when we know we are in the family of God. If we know we are in God's will, prayer becomes a demand, for we ask with the assurance that our demand will be fulfilled. We know we have it coming, because we are in the family.

Sometimes prayer requires us to fast, to abstain from food, because we cannot pray effectively with food on our mind. This is to be private fasting—no one is to know.

WHY PRAY?

Jesus said to pray all the time (*Luke 18:1–8*) so we do not

- Grow faint.

- Lose heart or give in to doubt, fear, or discouragement.

- Give up when prayer is not answered immediately.

- Fail to rebuke opposition.

- Resist the suggestion of failure.

- Forget we have a blood-bought right to an answer.

Prayer is imperative for communication with God. *Matthew 26:41*
We are commanded to watch and pray, so as not to yield to temptation.

Prayer is the only way to receive an answer from God. *James 4:2*

You do not have because you do not ask.

Prayer will save you out of all your troubles. *Psalm 34:6*

God will work to get us out of trouble and to deliver us from fears. *Psalm 34:4*

Prayer can unlock the treasure chest of God's wisdom. *James 1:5*

What any person lacks in knowledge, skill, and cleverness may be gained through prayer.

Prayer is a channel of power from God. *Jeremiah 33:3 NKJV*

"Call unto me and I will answer."

Jesus prayed often to the Father. *1 Thessalonians 5:17*

If the Son of God prayed, we should pray without ceasing.

To *Not* Pray Is a Sin

Displeasing the Lord by not praying is a sin because God commands us to pray. *1 Samuel 12:23*

Sinners are saved when they pray in faith. Believing in Christ and calling on Him in prayer presupposes faith in Him. *Romans 10:13–14*

Prayer is looking to God. There are three different ways to look:

- Within to be miserable *Psalm 77:1*

- Around to be distracted *Psalm 73:3*

- To God to be blessed *Psalm 34:5, Psalm 121:1*

How to Pray

The disciples wanted to learn to pray. They saw that Jesus' continued source of power and utter freedom from pride came through his secret prayer life. Jesus taught His disciples how to pray in *Luke 11:1*.

Pray to "our Father in heaven" because God is all loving, all wise, and all powerful. *Matthew 6:9*

Pray in the name of Jesus Christ. The Father is glorified through his Son. Jesus said, "Ask in my name and I will do it." *John 14:13–14*. Whatever the Father gives is in the name of Jesus. *John 16:23*

Pray with the help of the Holy Spirit. *Romans 8:26–27*. Our weakness causes us not to be able to form the words. The Holy Spirit takes the thoughts of our hearts, which is an intercession, and forms the words for us. Thus the jumbled thoughts of our hearts are turned into meaningful prayer.

Pray that God's will be done in everything. *James 4:15*. Do not plan for tomorrow without God. It is only if it's the Lord's will that we will even see tomorrow. Anything planned for tomorrow without the Lord's will is a form of boasting because we are stating that we will be here tomorrow when we really do not know that.

Pray for the coming of the kingdom at the Second Advent of Jesus because it will end sin's dominion on earth. We should want corruption to end and have an attitude of wanting to see sin end. *Matthew 25:31–46*

Pray for our daily necessities, day by day: food, clothes, shelter. *Luke 11:3*. We pray for everything that concerns us in life.

Pray and give thanks for everything. *Philippians 4:6–7*

Pray for forgiveness. *Matthew 18:21–22*

Pray for grace to forgive, so that we may be forgiven. *2 Corinthians 12:7–10*. Forgiveness must be practiced just as prayer is practiced. Forgiving others is the condition of God's forgiveness of us. We are to forgive an infinite number of times. We are to forgive our habitual trespassers and persecutors. *Romans 12:14*

Pray for the leading of the Lord. *Luke 22:42*. We ask the Lord to lead us, to direct our path, and deliver us from evil. *Psalm 23*. When we get off the path, we ask God to put us back on it. We do not wait for someone else to pray for us. We say, "Lord, You know that down in my heart I do not want to do evil, so when I am tempted by evil, get me away from it."

Pray in faith. *Hebrews 11:6*. It is impossible to please God without faith. Without faith there is no real belief that God exists. Without belief in the existence of God, our prayers are not answered.

The model prayer in *Luke 11* is the perfect prayer because it is

- Brief

- To the point

- Not repetitious

WHERE TO PRAY

Pray in all places and at all times. *Ephesians 6:18*
Paul and Silas prayed in prison! *Acts 16:25*
Pray when assembled with believers. *Acts 1:13–14*
Pray when you go from place to place. *1 Timothy 2:8*
The most important place to pray is anywhere you can be alone with God. *Matthew 6:6*

It is a great joy to be able to talk with God anytime, any-place, under any condition and to know God will hear and answer.

UNANSWERED PRAYER

When your prayers are not answered, examine yourself according to God's Word. If in this self-analysis something not pleasing to God is found, confess it and believe God will forgive. Once cleansed, your prayers may be answered.

Hindrances to prayer:

- Lack of oneness between husband and wife. Many prayers go unanswered because of the unfaithfulness of husbands and wives. *1 Peter 3:1–7*

- Selfishness, asking for things that our own lusts may be satisfied. *James 4:3*

- Wrong done to others or having an unforgiving spirit when wronged. *Matthew 5:22, 24*. Humble yourself and seek reconciliation if you are angry without a just cause. *Matthew 5:22*. If your cause for anger is just, keep your temper under strict control. *Ephesians 4:26, Galatians 5:22*

- Unbelief. *James 1:6–7*. Prayer is only answered to the extent one believes. A doubter, who one minute believes and the next does not, will not have prayer answered.

- Sin in the heart. *Isaiah 59:1–2*. Sin builds a wall between God and a person who has not confessed that sin to God. It cuts off communication.

- Asking with wrong motives. *James 4:3*. Do not be afraid to ask. There is joy in prayer. *John 16:24*. Simply ask in faith and you will receive. We are

not limited to asking for salvation. Jesus said, "Any and all things will be given in My name."
John 14:12–15

For answered prayer, earnestly believe God will hear and answer.

DOES GOD ANSWER ALL PRAYER?

God answers all prayer, but does not say yes to all requests. Sometimes God says wait and sometimes no. The answer is sometimes different than expected. We must consider our relationship with God in order to properly understand God's answers.

Once you are born again, you *abide* in Christ. To abide is to be satisfied with the consequences of conforming to God's Word. *John 15:7*

If you abide in Christ, you will bear fruit of the Spirit. If you stop abiding in Christ, if you do not conform after being born again, you will not grow, and your prayers will not be answered because you will have no relationship with God for the answers to come through. The all-inclusive condition to answered prayer is abiding in Christ. As you abide in Christ, ask what you will and it shall be done.

Answers are sometimes immediate. When Peter walked

on water toward Jesus, as he sank he prayed, "Lord, save me!" The answer was immediate—he was saved. *Matthew 14:22–31*

Answers are sometimes delayed and provided according to God's timing. *Romans 8:28.* Jesus was sent for when Lazarus was sick, but Jesus delayed and Lazarus died. However, Jesus raised Lazarus from the dead. *John 11:1–44.* The answer was delayed but not denied.

Answers are sometimes no. *Mark 14:36, Matthew 26:42.* When the Lord answers with a no, it is accompanied with peace.

God answers all Christian prayers, not according to our wishes but according to God's perfect will.

THE LORD'S PRAYER

The Lord's Prayer is a model for praying, a framework on which we build our prayer life. The starting point is to learn the model prayer, get to know the various parts, and then build from there. Knowing the different elements is important. *Matthew 6:9–13, Mark 11:25–26, Luke 11:2–4*

> "Our Father"—Establishing the relationship; this is a salutation to God, recognizing who He is and whose we are.

"Which art in heaven"—Recognition; this identifies
the God to whom we are praying.

"Hallowed be thy Name"—Adoration; we start out
adoring God, saying thank you, and giving praise.

"Thy kingdom come"—Anticipation of the coming of
Christ's Second Advent and submission; this is a
declaration of God's rule in our lives.

"Thy will be done"—Consecration: "I am at Your
disposal, Father God"; "I am ready for whatever
You have in store for me."

"On earth"—Universality; this is recognizing the
universal power of God.

"As it is in heaven"—Conformity; as the angels and
inhabitants of heaven do God's will, I give over my
complete will to God in the same way.

FAITH

And without faith it is impossible to please God,
because anyone who comes to him
must believe that he exists
and that he rewards those who earnestly seek him.

Hebrews 11:6 NIV

A number of definitions have been used to explain faith. Even so, we still struggle with attempts to explain faith.

Faith is the assurance, or title deed, to eternal life and more. *Hebrews 11:1–3*

Just as a deed is evidence of title in real estate, so faith is evidence of title in the estate of God.

Faith is trust when walking in or toward an unknown future. *Hebrews 11:8–10*

Faith is believing God and asking no questions. *Hebrews 11:6*

Faith is knowing that God causes all things (good or bad) to work together for good for those who love the Lord and are obedient to divine purpose. *Romans 8:28*

Faith has two sides: intellect and will.

With the intellect, we have the conviction that Jesus Christ is God. We surrender our will to Jesus Christ. Thomas said of the resurrected Jesus, "My Lord and my God." *John 20:28 NIV.* "My Lord" indicates volitional surrender. "My God" shows intellectual conviction.

We are not born with faith. Faith comes from hearing the Word of God. *Romans 10:17 By our will, we choose to accept what we hear.* Faith goes beyond reasoning. Faith believes without totally understanding why. Our faith honors God, and God always honors faith.

IMPORTANCE OF FAITH

In *Ephesians 6:10–18*, Paul names the different parts of the Christian armor.

He puts special emphasis on the shield of faith. *Ephesians 6:16.* With the shield of faith, nothing can hurt you. The shield is like a door that a soldier hides behind.

We cannot be saved without faith. *John 3:3, Ephesians 2:8, Romans 1:17*

Faith empowers us to live victoriously. *1 John 5:4*

The faithful suffer persecution and receive blessings. Trials perfect our faith. *2 Corinthians 13:5*. They make us more settled or grounded. *2 Corinthians 6:4–8*

We cannot please God without faith. *Hebrews 11:6*. For an illustration of different types of faith in action read *Hebrews 11*.

Belief is the act and process of faith. *Acts 14:21–22*. It is the present tense of faith. We must continue in belief to receive the benefits of faith.

Without faith, prayer is not effective. *James 1:6*

Without faith we cannot have peace with God. *Romans 5:1*

Faith gives us justification for peace. We are justified by faith, not works. *Galatians 2:16*

With faith and peace we experience joy. *1 Peter 1:8*

With faith we can live in peace. *Galatians 2:20*

We are made righteous by faith. *Habakkuk 2:4, Romans 10:1–4*

We receive the Holy Spirit through faith. *Galatians 3:2*

Whatever is not from faith is sin. *Romans 14:23*

THREE KINDS OF FAITH

Martha, the sister of Lazarus illustrates the three kinds of faith. Jesus arrived at the gravesite of Lazarus to raise

102 ⟶ ABCs of Christianity

him up. Martha met him there and exhibited the three kinds of faith. *John 11:21–44*

Limited Faith

Martha said, "My brother would not have died if you had been here." *John 11:21 NIV*

Her faith ended with Lazarus' death. She believed Christ could make her brother well if he was sick, but she did not consider that Jesus had power over death. Her limited faith restricted the power of Jesus. *Matthew 13:58*

Limited faith is controlled by circumstances. It is motivated by fear of failure. Unbelief limits power—if there is no faith, there can be no miracle.

Fundamental Faith

Jesus said, "Your brother shall rise again." *John 11:23 NIV*

When Martha responded, "I know he will rise in the resurrection" (*John 11:24 NIV*), she showed her fundamental faith, which was not enough because Jesus told her that He had power over life and death (*John 11:25*) and asked her, "Do you believe this?" *John 11:26 NIV*

Martha answered, "I believe you are the Messiah, the Son of God, who is to come into the world." *John 11:27 NIV*

That is the fundamental faith creed, a shallow answer

that evaded the question. Martha made a true statement, answering something that was not asked. Fundamental faith is not enough—it limits the power of Christ. To do the work of God, our faith must exceed fundamental faith. Fundamental faith just gets us started.

Unlimited Faith

Martha showed unbelief when she refused to have the stone removed from Lazarus' grave.

She made excuses: "He stinks." *John 11:39 KJV*

Jesus said, "If you believe you will see the glory of God." *John 11:40 NIV*

Jesus challenged Martha to believe. Martha consented to having the stone moved from the grave. Martha's faith no longer limited the power of God.

We must move the stones away in our lives to see the glory of God. We must have unlimited faith and not be satisfied with limited or fundamental faith. We can strive to attain unlimited faith that pleases God and reveals the Lord's glory.

THE RIGHTEOUS SHALL LIVE BY FAITH

This is stated four times in the Bible.
Habakkuk 2:4, Galatians 3:10–11, Romans 1:17, Hebrews 10:38

The lives of the righteous and the unrighteous are different.

The Unrighteous

- Have confidence in themselves.

- Are purposeless.

- Transgress because of habits.

- Do evil shamelessly.

- Covet because of greed.

- Lust and are never satisfied.

The Righteous

- Live by faith and the principles of faith.

- Have confidence in God.

- Have faith that is more than a philosophy.

- Are saved by faith.

- Maintain faith.

Righteous faith will be tried and proven by trials many times and in many ways. *1 Peter 1:7*

People of genuine faith know how to wait on the Lord. They do not give up; they hang in there and resist temptation, knowing that God is coming. *Isaiah 40:31*

Faith is always victorious. Our faith can overcome the world! *1 John 5:4*

Faith defies reason and moves mountains. *Matthew 17:14–21*

Faith does not mean that all things work out well. Faith does not make anything easy, but it does make all things possible. *Hebrews 11:32–39*

THE HALL OF FAITH

Read *Hebrews 11:32–39*, the Hall of Faith. The heroes of faith are similar to our Halls of Fame that feature giants in sports. By reading the exploits of those in the Hall of Faith, our faith may become stronger in the Lord. The heroes demonstrate the power of faith:

Moses—faith's protection *Exodus 12*
Israel—faith's preservation *Exodus 14:15–31*
Gideon—faith's miraculous victory *Judges 6:18*
Rahab—faith's deliverance *Joshua 2:1, 9, 11*
Barak—faith's triumph *Judges 4–5*
Samson—faith's physical strength *Judges 13:1–16*
Jephthah—faith's boldness *Judges 11:1–12*

David—faith's utter reliance on God
   1 Samuel 17:32–51
Samuel—faith's integrity *1 Samuel 3:18, 7:1–17, 8:1–3*

Only by faith in the power of Jesus Christ can we be superior to circumstances and be victorious over all the forces that would destroy us. Jesus is the author of and the perfecter of our faith. *Hebrews 12:2.* We look to the faith of saints for inspiration, but we look to Jesus as our example of faith.

THE ABUNDANT LIFE

*"I came that they may have life
and have it abundantly."*

John 10:10 ESV

S ome believers think the only benefit to following Christ is eternal life. There is more! Christ came that we may have life abundantly once we accept Jesus as our Savior right now, right here on earth.

The abundant life is a mature Christian life. To reach maturity as Christians, we must grow. Every day, Christians should draw closer to Christ. Our maturity depends on becoming more like Christ. Scriptures give us the stages of spiritual growth in the Christian life. *2 Peter 3:18*

THE BABY STAGE

The baby stage is the beginning of Christian living. *1 Corinthians 3:1–4*

A baby is selfish, gets upset if denied desires, seeks its own, feels hurt easily, is often jealous, lives to be served, never wants to serve unselfishly, drinks milk but cannot eat meat, cries but very seldom, if ever, sings, and tries to talk but does not make sense.

The above infant characteristics are prominent in many Church members. They have been born into the family of God but have failed to develop spiritually. They are carnal Christians.

Baby Christians can be recognized by

- Envy—state of the mind

- Strife—contention in words

- Deeds—sin in conduct

THE CHILD STAGE

The next stage of Christian maturity is the child stage. *1 John 2:12*

The child is untruthful, envious, cruel, and repeats everything. (In adults, it is called gossip.) If rebuked, the child becomes a martyr who feels picked on. The child is given to emotional outbursts, if crossed is resentful, and often makes a scene. The child is easily puffed up and loves praise from any source. The child seeks only what appeals to self.

Those in this stage of Christian life aren't mature enough to withstand a strong attack of sin or to fight off errors in teaching or doctrine. They cannot tell when a doctrine is counterfeit. Only those who are experienced in Christian living and teaching can detect such errors. *Ephesians 4:14*

THE YOUNG ADULT STAGE

These Christians have grown to the prime of spiritual life. *1 John 2:13–14.* A young adult is strong in the Lord (*Ephesians 6:10*), able to overcome sin, has a vision for his or her future, courageously tackles that vision, and prepares for productive years. They are no longer swayed by fallacies. Becoming a young adult spiritually takes putting away childish things. *1 Corinthians 13:11*

THE ADULT (MATURE) STAGE

The adult, or mature, stage of Christian spiritual development can be reached by all, but only a few attain it. The adult has peace with God (*Romans 5:1*), is not at war within or with God, and is secure in being justified by faith through Jesus Christ. The adult experiences the peace of God during the storms of life (*Philippians 4:7, John 16:33*), rejoices in spiritual children (those brought to Christ) (*1 Thessalonians 2:19, 1 Timothy 1:2*), and has learned to be content under all circumstances. *Philippians 4:6–11*

Mature Christians know the source of true strength (*Philippians 4:13*) and do not brood over the past but instead look to the future (*Philippians 3:13–14*), knowing that all things, both good and bad incidents, work together in their lives for their eternal good. *Romans 8:28*

Mature Christians enjoy the abundant life now and will enjoy the life to come. *Mark 10:29, Ephesians 2:7*

ABUNDANT LIFE REVIEW

The abundant life is not based on material resources.

The abundant life is a life of spiritual depth.

Jesus Christ controls our abundant life.

The abundant life is a life of service. We serve God by doing what Jesus Christ would do.

The abundant life is a life separated from sin.

A Christian reaches maturity when he or she can say, "It is no longer I, but Christ who lives in me." *Galatians 2:20 NKJV*

When we are mature Christians, doing God's will, not our childish will, becomes our conduct. Christ's character shows in believers who are living the abundant life.

THE NEW BIRTH

*Jesus answered, "Very truly I tell you, no one
can enter the kingdom of God unless they are
born of water and the Spirit. Flesh gives birth
to flesh, but the Spirit gives birth to spirit."*

John 3:5–6 NIV

What does "born again" actually mean? We study the
new birth to understand what Jesus meant when He said
to Nicodemus, "You must be born again." *John 3:1–8 NIV*

Nicodemus was a ruler, one of the richest men in
Jerusalem, and a very religious man. Meeting him
face-to-face, Jesus told Nicodemus that his religion was
not enough. Nicodemus needed regeneration; he needed
life. Jesus told him, in order to have life, "you must be
born again." *John 3:3*

The difference is between a flesh birth and a spiritual birth. *John 3:6*

The new birth is a spiritual birth. It is an actual birth of the spirit, similar to a natural birth, but a birth of the spirit and not the flesh. The new birth is not a figure of speech.

The only way to become a child of God is to be born again. You cannot become a child of God by joining a church.

Spiritual birth is from God. *1 Peter 1:23*

The agents of the new birth are the Holy Spirit (*John 3:6*), and the Word of God. *1 Peter 1:23*

The new birth makes the believer a new creation in Christ. *2 Corinthians 5:17*

It is a spiritual resurrection. *Ephesians 2:1–9*

It is a regeneration or renewal where sins and wrong-doing no longer matter to God and the Holy Spirit makes it possible for us to conquer the urge to commit those old wrongs. *Titus 3:5*

God allows us in the new birth to partake of the divine nature. *2 Peter 1:4*

The new birth comes when faith is placed in Jesus Christ as Savior and Lord. *John 1:12*

GOD'S PLAN OF SALVATION

*And this is the testimony: God has given
us eternal life, and this life is in his Son.
Whoever has the Son has life; whoever does
not have the Son of God does not have life.*

1 John 5:11–12 NIV

All are God's creation, but only God's plan can make
one a child of God. *Acts 4:12*

Not all religions lead to God. God's way is through
the person of Jesus Christ. No other name can save.
John 14:6

Jesus said He was the way to God (*Matthew 7:14*) and
the truth of God. *1 John 5:20*

Jesus is the source of eternal life, the living way to God, the author of eternal salvation. *Hebrews 5:9, 10:20*

What Salvation Means

Through salvation, we are saved from the penalty of sin, the power of sin, and the presence of sin.

Power of Sin

Christ died so we do not have to suffer the penalty for our wrongs. *Hebrews 9:26*

Jesus Christ appeared in heaven after resurrection to save us from the power our sins have to convict us. *Hebrews 9:24*

Penalty of Sin

Christ is in heaven representing us, reminding God that He has paid the penalty. He is our Advocate with the Father. *1 John 2:1–2*

Presence of Sin

Jesus will appear on earth again to rid us from the very presence of sin. He will come not as a sacrifice but to rule a sin-free world. *Hebrews 9:28*

God Loves Us

God gave His Son so the world could be saved. God's love is everlasting, fathomless, and indescribable. *John 3:16*

Jesus' coming is expressive of the concept and magnitude of God's love. He came to redeem us by God's will—humans had nothing to do with it. *John 1:13–14*

Christ Died for Our Salvation

Christ died for all sinners, that is, all of us. *Romans 5:6–8*

Christ, who did not sin, was made sin for us that we may become right with God. *2 Corinthians 5:21*

Jesus Christ rose bodily from the grave, opening the way for us to have eternal life.
Psalm 16:10, Psalm 22:1, John 11:25, 1 Corinthians 6:14

We Are Saved by Faith in Jesus Christ

In order to be saved, we must believe the following *1 Corinthians 15:3–4*:

- Christ died for our sins.

- He was buried.

- He rose on the third day.

- Jesus is our Advocate in heaven.

A formal mental acceptance of Jesus is not enough. We must surrender all to God. An act of faith is necessary for salvation: We must not be ashamed of the Gospel. *Romans 1:16*

We must verbally claim the Lord Jesus Christ as our Savior and believe that God raised Him from the dead. *Romans 10:9–10*

Those words and faith guarantee salvation.

This is a sample prayer to be prayed at the time of repentance:

> *Lord Jesus, I know You love me because*
> *You died on the cross bearing my sins.*
> *Thank You, Lord, for revealing to me my*
> *lost, sinful condition. I confess that I am a*
> *sinner, I am dead in sin, and I cannot save*
> *myself. I do now by faith gladly accept You*
> *as my personal Savior, and thank You,*
> *Lord, for eternal salvation. Amen.*

You Can Know You Are Saved

The Bible helps you know that you have eternal life. Every believer has a personal witness from God to their faith. *1 John 5:10–13*

Remember, God cannot deny His Word or Himself. *Numbers 23:19, John 14:1–2, Romans 4:7, Hebrews 11:6*

God would have you know that you are now (once you are born again) a child of God. *1 John 3:2*

You can know that you are a new person in Christ. *2 Corinthians 5:17*

All the above is promised by the infallible Word of God. Heaven and earth may pass away, but His Word shall never pass away. *Matthew 24:35*

Salvation Stirs Obedience

Salvation requires obedience. *Acts 5:29*

To be salvaged from sin is to take on the character of Christ. Now you are a child of God.

Unite with a New Testament church. *Acts 2:47*

Get water baptized. *Acts 2:41, 8:34–40.* Baptism will let the world know you are set apart. Baptism is an outward manifestation that you have been born again. It is telling the world you have a new and clean heart (become new, act new). Remember: Baptism does not save. It is a witness that you believe in the death, burial, and resurrection of Christ. *Romans 6:4*

Attend worship services and join a Bible study group. *Hebrews 10:25.* Staying home and watching church on TV or by live-streaming will not do.

Make time in your routine for daily prayer and reading the Word of God.

Pray that you may grow and really know Jesus Christ. The more you know about God, the more your aim should be to please your new Savior.

Seven facts are revealed in God's plan of salvation:

- God loves us. *John 3:16*

- We are all sinners. *Romans 3:9, 23*

- We are now dead to sin. *Romans 6:23*

- Christ died for us. *Romans 5:6–8*

- We are saved by faith in Jesus Christ. *Acts 16:30–31*

- You can know that you are saved. *1 John 5:10–13*

- Salvation commands action. *Acts 5:29*

GLOSSARY

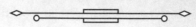

abomination: Actions or deeds that are deemed an abomination are actions that are detestable to God. This term especially applies to idolatry or putting other things before God.

agape: Much of the New Testament portion of the Bible was written in the Greek language and it has many words distinguishing the various kinds of love. (In the English language, we use the same word to specify different kinds of love.) Among the Greek words for love are *eros* (erotic love); *phileo* (camaraderie or brotherly love); and agape. In the New Testament, agape is the Greek word used to designate the perfect, unconditional love God has for humanity. This same love moved Christ to die on the cross for our sin.

air, "in the air": The space above the earth where Christ will return to reign, where He will be visible to all. The Bible does not indicate that Christ will come all the way to earth when He returns, but He can be seen in the air. His saints will meet Him in the air and He will take them with Him.

Almighty: One of God's titles. In the Hebrew language, which is the primary language of the Old Testament, "Almighty" is translated from *El Shaddai*. This title is also used in the New Testament several times to refer to God, just as one might refer to a physician simply as "Doctor" or "Doc." The title expresses that there is none greater than the God who created the first man and woman and who made an everlasting promise to Abraham, Isaac, and Jacob.

altar of the Lord: Where human beings connect with God. A special place reserved to worship and make intimate connection with God. A holy place designated for worship, sacrifice, confession, prayer, and praise. In the Old Testament, the altar most often refers to an actual altar that was built out in the open, or in the Temple or synagogue as a special place to connect to God. Although some Christians may establish a private altar in their home, we establish communion with God in the altar of our hearts.

amillennialism: This belief rejects the interpretation of the book of Revelation that Christ will return and reign on earth for a thousand years.

apostle: The term is applied to the twelve disciples who engaged in Jesus' public ministry on earth. When they were in need of a replacement apostle, the qualifications for apostle was clear: one who had participated in Jesus' earthly ministry,

beginning with his baptism, and had witnessed his
resurrection.

apostle Paul: Originally named Saul of Tarsus, he was a
Jewish man, highly trained in his religion, who hated
and persecuted followers of Jesus. He later converted,
accepting Jesus as Lord and Savior. Although he had
not witnessed Jesus' baptism or resurrection, Saul,
who was later named Paul, introduced himself in his
letters to the churches as an apostle, an appointment
given to him by God's authority. Paul was the
greatest single contributor to the New Testament
writings. It is generally accepted that he wrote
thirteen letters (epistles) that are part of the Bible.

Apostolic Benediction: The closing found in
2 Corinthians 13:14. Some variation of these words is
used by many churches at the close of their worship
service.

Apostolic Church: The first church, which was
established by the apostles. This church is sometimes
referred to as the Early Church or the Jerusalem
Church or the Mother Church.

ascension: When resurrected Christ returned to God in
heaven.

atonement: In the Old Testament, an act of
reconciliation, performed by the blood sacrifice of
animals as an offering to God to remove the effects
of sin. In the New Testament, atonement refers to

the reconciliation between God and humanity made possible by the death, burial, and resurrection of Christ.

author (of our faith): A metaphor meaning Jesus Christ is the reason for our faith.

backslide: When Christians stop doing the things Christ has commanded. They do not stop believing in God; however, they may engage in activities that are contrary to the teachings of Christ.

baptism of believers: Baptism is one of the two generally accepted ordinances (acts commanded by Christ) of the Church. The other is Communion. Those who openly put faith in Jesus Christ as the one sent to earth by God to save humanity from sin are baptized by being dipped or sprinkled with water as an act of obedience and a public affirmation of faith.

Bible scrolls: The various ancient manuscripts from which the Bible is compiled. The biblical texts were originally written on scrolls.

Bible translation: The original manuscripts from which the Bible is compiled were written in ancient Hebrew, Greek, and Aramaic. All of these languages have been translated into English. Translations include the King James Version, written in seventeenth-century English, and the contemporary-language translations of today. Bibles that summarize the ideas, rather than translating the actual words, and use current cultural examples, words, and illustrations are "paraphrases" rather than translations.

blood-bought: The benefits to those who believe Jesus' crucifixion absolves them of sin before God.

blood-washed believer: A term to acknowledge that a believer's salvation is made possible by the personal sacrifice of Jesus' blood on the cross. In the Old Testament, the Israelites made blood sacrifices to God as an attempt to be reconciled after separation because of sin. This sacrifice had to be made over and over again. Jesus is our once-and-for all blood sacrifice for the sins of humanity. See *Ephesians 1:7.*

body of Christ: The Church, meaning all those who claim Jesus Christ as Lord and Savior and who work in service to Him.

born again: The spiritual life that begins when you believe in Jesus Christ, repent of personal sin, and accept that Jesus' sacrificial death on the cross connects you to God.

the bread and wine: The two elements used to observe the ordinance of the Lord's Supper. This is also the meal Jesus shared with disciples before his arrest, crucifixion, and resurrection. These elements are chosen because they were also partaken during the Passover, when God miraculously orchestrated the release of the Hebrew people from slavery in Egypt.

Calvary: The location just outside the city walls of ancient Jerusalem where Jesus was crucified.

caught up: See **rapture**.

chastening: The disciplinary acts of God upon humanity.

Church/church: When written with a capital letter, the term refers to the universal Church, all churches everywhere that minister under the authority of Jesus Christ. When written with a lowercase letter, the term refers to a local body of believers.

Communion: The act of eating bread made without yeast (unleavened) and drinking a small cup of juice or wine to remember and honor the sacrifice Jesus made when He died on the cross. The cup represents the shed blood of Jesus. The bread represents His body. Taking communion is one of the two generally accepted ordinances (acts commanded by Christ) of the Church. The other is baptism. Communion is sometimes referred to as the Lord's Supper or the Eucharist.

conversion: Turning to a life lived without God to one lived in obedience to God as a follower of Jesus Christ.

court of heaven: To paint His disciples a word picture of how prayer is entertained in heaven, Jesus used the context of a courtroom. When we pray, God is the judge and Christ intercedes on our behalf, as would a defense lawyer in a courtroom. The resurrected Jesus is seated at the right hand of the Father, the righteous Judge, continuously interceding for grace, mercy, and blessings on our behalf. See *Luke 18:1–8, Hebrews 4:15–16.*

credited writers: Those human beings divinely chosen to be contributing writers of the Bible. They personally witnessed God operating in human history.

crown of life: The New Testament mentions five types of crowns, each representing a reward for a special act of service or faithfulness within the Kingdom of God. They are the everlasting crown (*1 Corinthians 9:25*); the crown for the one who wins souls (*Philippians 4:1, 1 Thessalonians 2:19*); the crown of righteousness (*2 Timothy 4:8*); the crown of glory (*1 Peter 5:4*); and the crown of life (*James 1:12, Revelation 2:10*). The crown of life is given to those who faithfully persist through trials, temptations, and persecutions.

deacons: Derived from the Greek word *diakonos,* which is usually understood to mean "servant." The first deacons were chosen and set apart to serve the needy in their community.

disciple: A follower Jesus Christ. Jesus had many followers. The Bible often highlights the ministry of the twelve who were a part of His inner circle. They are also known as apostles.

dominion: Power, authority, or control over a territory or entity. Upon His resurrection, all authority over heaven and earth was given to Jesus, the Christ. See *Matthew 28:18–20*

early Church: The organized assemblage of Christ's disciples during the first three hundred years after His resurrection.

emblems: Symbols that illustrate the Christian faith or refer to God, Christ, and the Holy Spirit.

the enemy: Satan is the enemy of God and God's people. Satan opposes, accuses, tests, and slanders believers. The enemy opposes God's word, God's purposes, and God's righteousness. He is the adversary because he deceives and is the father of lies. See *John 8:44*.

epistles: The letters that comprise most of the New Testament. The English word "epistle" is used to refer to written correspondence.

established, self-governing branch of the Christian Church: Followers of Jesus organized on certain theological, doctrinal, and sometimes cultural beliefs.

evangelist: A Christian who shares the Gospel in various places outside a local church. Evangelists may share the good news about the saving power of Jesus Christ with unbelievers locally, nationally, or internationally.

evangelize: Sharing the life, ministry, crucifixion, and resurrection of Christ with those who do not yet believe. Jesus gave the command to every believer to go out and make disciples. See *Matthew 28:19–20*.

false doctrine: Untrue teachings about the Bible, God, Jesus Christ, or the Holy Spirit. During the early days of Christianity, many false prophets arose and distorted the teachings of Christ. Most untruths are asserted for the benefit of the one telling them.

fast: A period of abstinence from a substance or activity in order to spend that time to deepen one's relationship with God or to gain spiritual insight. Believers most often abstain from food, but may abstain from drinking certain beverages, sexual activity, or even television or social media.

finisher (of our faith): Our faith is made complete in Jesus Christ through his crucifixion and resurrection.

first estate, leaving: The perfect habitat of angels and celestial beings from which Satan and his followers were cast out after they rebelled against God.

Gentiles: All persons not born of Jewish ancestry. The term is used to designate those who do not believe in or follow God.

God hates: God is love, and always loves humanity, but despises the evil deeds humans sometimes commit. God hates sin, but never stops loving the people who commit them.

Godhead: A term used to describe the holy Trinity—
God in three persons: Creator, Redeemer, and Spirit;
or Father, Son, and Holy Ghost.

God's Word of truth: The Bible. All of the decrees, acts,
deeds, and commands contained therein are from God.

the Gospel: The detailed account of God's activity on
behalf of humanity through the life, ministry, death,
and resurrection of Jesus. In the Great Commission
(*Matthew 28:19–20*), Jesus instructs His disciples to go
and share the Gospel message all over the world.

Great Commission: The command given by the
resurrected Christ to His disciples to go through the
world and baptize, make disciples, and teach them
about the ministry and teachings of Christ. This
commission is found in *Matthew 28:19–20*.

Great White Throne Judgment: This is the final
judgment, which is upon unbelievers before they
are thrown into the lake of fire for eternity. See
Revelation 20:11–15.

Greek: The original language of most of the New
Testament writings. The majority of the New
Testament was written in Greek or Aramaic.

Hades: A Greek word meaning the place of the dead,
which appears as *sheol* in the Old Testament. Usually
translated as "hell." The most precise translation for
hell, the place of eternal punishment, is the Greek
word *Gehenna*.

Hall of Faith: The faithful men and women of the Bible who are hailed in *Hebrews 11* for their perseverance, obedience, and devotion to God.

Hebrew: The original language of most of the Old Testament writings.

Hebrew, Greek, and Aramaic: These are the three languages in which the most authentic biblical manuscripts are written.

Helper: A term often used to describe the work and purpose of the Holy Spirit. Jesus asked God to send us a Helper who would come after the crucifixion as an ongoing presence in the lives of His followers. The Helper would guide the disciples to all truth. This Helper is still available to guide believers today. The Helper first came upon Jesus' followers in *Acts 2:1–4*.

imperishable wreath: A metaphor of Olympic champions to help Christ followers understand what we should strive for. The Olympic athletics worked hard and trained in order to receive a prize that amounted to a laurel made of leaves that would die in a few days. Believers do work to obtain the wreath that cannot die or be destroyed—heaven, after our earthly life.

iniquity: Most often translated from the Greek word *anomia*, which refers to "lawlessness" and is used as a general description of sinful behavior or action that opposes the righteousness of God.

inspired: God chose persons to write the biblical accounts and directed them in doing so.

Israel: The name has many meanings in the Bible: (1) Israel is the nation of people descended from Abraham. (2) It refers to those God chose to have a special relationship with. (3) Jacob is often called Israel. (4) In the New Testament, Israel is used to refer to the Church, the body of Christ. Those under the Lordship of Christ become a part of Israel as a continuation of God's work in the Old Testament to relate to obedient and faithful people.

Jews: Hebrew people (also called Israelites). It is a derivative of Judah, the name of one of the twelve tribes of Hebrew people. Judah was the largest tribe.

John the Baptist: An unconventional Jew who told people that Jesus, the Messiah (Savior), was coming. He encouraged people to repent (turn from sin) and baptized them in water. See *Matthew 3:11*.

judgment seat of Christ: During New Testament times, one in authority occupied a specific seat to render judgment on issues. After his arrest, Jesus was brought before Pontius Pilate, who straddled a raised platform from which he dispensed the judgment that Jesus would be crucified. Paul was also brought before a judgment seat at the city of Corinth. The judgment seat that Christ will occupy upon His return is where He will dispense the ruling every human being must face on Judgment Day.

justified/justification: God cannot relate to sin. Humans are sinful. In order to be restored to a right relationship with God, Jesus took the punishment for our sin, and our sin is no longer viewed by God. God can relate to us. We are seen as right or "just" in God's eyes because of Jesus. We cannot be justified by following the law (doing everything right). Only through Christ can humans relate to a righteous God. See *Acts 13:39, Romans 5:9, Galatians 3:24.*

the kingdom: The kingdom of God represents the dominion of God over all things. Nothing on earth or in the heavens is outside of God's authority. Jesus spoke often about God's kingdom and the role of believers in it.

Law, Law of Moses: Contained in the first five books of the Old Testament, also known as the Pentateuch and the Torah, these are the laws Moses brought to the people of Israel. These laws served as their guide for holy living.

living Christ (Savior): Refers to the resurrected Jesus, who rose from the dead, was taken up to heaven, and is with God as an advocate for all believers. See *Acts 2:33.*

The Lord's Supper: See **Communion**.

the lost: Those who have no relationship with God through faith in Jesus Christ. Jesus declared that He came to save the lost. See *Luke 19:10.*

missionaries: Persons who are commissioned by a church or other established religious entity to share the Gospel with those who have not heard it or to provide aid as the Gospel is shared.

the new birth: The new life that believers have through faith in Christ. Jesus said that unless we experience a new birth, we cannot see the kingdom of heaven. *John 3:3.* The new birth is symbolized via baptism with water.

New Testament: The second section of the Christian Bible, comprised of twenty-seven books. It details God's work to establish fellowship with humanity through Jesus Christ and the Creator's plan to ensure that this unbroken divine-human relationship will last into eternity.

Old Testament: The first section of the Christian Bible, comprised of thirty-nine books. It contains God's laws, along with the history of God's many attempts to establish an unbroken relationship with humanity. These books of the Bible detail a relationship with God based on God's law, which human beings cannot permanently uphold. For those of the Jewish faith, the Old Testament is the complete Bible.

ordinances of the Church: The Christian Church observes two religious rites as commanded by Christ. (1) Baptism (see *Matthew 28:19*) is a public demonstration of faith in Jesus. (2) The Lord's Supper or Communion (see *I Corinthians 11:23-26)* is the regular partaking of a small amount of wine or juice and unyeasted bread to remember the sacrifice Jesus made for us. Some churches believe that washing feet is also an ordinance. In *John 13:14*, after Jesus had washed the feet of the twelve disciples, He encouraged them to wash each other's feet. Most churches that hold foot-washing ceremonies do so as an act of humility and service, but not as an ordinance.

Paraclete: Greek name for the Holy Spirit. It literally means "one called alongside." Paraclete is often translated as "advocate." Jesus asked God to send the Holy Spirit to His believers so they would have a comforter and a helper who would always be with them after His crucifixion and resurrection.

Passover: A major Jewish holiday/festival that commemorates God's miraculous deliverance of the Israelites from slavery. The festival lasts for seven or eight days. Easter is always connected to the timing of Passover, since Jesus ate his last meal with his disciples during that festival time.

Paul: See **apostle Paul**.

Pentecost, day of: The day the Holy Spirit first appeared to believers after Jesus' resurrection. Pentecost is from a Greek word meaning "fifty," because the Holy Spirit came upon believers fifty days after Passover. See *Acts 2*.

perfecter: The King James Version of the Bible translates the Greek word *teleiōtēn* used in *Hebrews 12:2* as "finisher." God makes faith complete. In this verse, faith is analogous to competitive games. As the perfecter of faith, God alone has the authority to award the prize for our faithfulness to God through Jesus Christ.

Pharisees: The largest and most influential Jewish religious-political body of the New Testament era. They were well versed in the Torah (the laws and instructions given to Moses). They often took issue with the teaching of Jesus, who was also Jewish, and Jesus often condemned their practices as hypocrisy.

postmillennialism: An interpretation of scripture that Christ will return to earth and rule after the entire earth has been converted to Christianity by his followers. This period is possibly one thousand years.

premillennialism: An interpretation of scripture that Christ will return to earth and establish his rule by overtaking the forces that are hostile to God. This era of Christ's rule will possibly last for one thousand years.

prince of the power of the air: A term used to describe the capabilities of Satan in *Ephesians 2:2*.

publican: A political position established by the Roman government to collect taxes. Those who held this position were especially despised because they were viewed as extortionists who levied heavy taxes against citizens to include a hefty profit for themselves. Most tax collectors were Romans, but Jewish tax collectors were especially despised by other Jews because they were viewed as traitors. The term is found primarily in the King James Version of the Bible.

rapture: Believers living at the time of Christ's return to earth will be taken up in the air to meet Him. See *1 Thessalonians 4:17.*

redemption: In its original context, the process involved in paying the price required to obtain the release of a convicted criminal. Biblical writers widely used the concept to describe God's work to save humanity from sin and its consequences. Jesus' sacrifice of His life on the cross was payment, redeeming sinful human beings.

regenerates believers: The process of renewal that occurs in the lives of believers as Christ takes them from an old, sinful way of life to new life in Him.

repentance: An intentional turning away from sin toward God. This spiritual redirection is usually accompanied by genuine sorrow for past deeds, with resolve to live differently.

reprove: To reprimand, discipline, chastise, or instruct regarding wrongdoing.

resurrection: The miraculous act of coming from death back to life.

revealed Word of God: This phrase can be understood to mean the Bible or it can refer to Jesus, who is also called the Word in *John 1*.

revile: To criticize in an excessive, cruel, or abusive manner.

the righteousness of God: Either "God gives righteousness" or "God is righteousness." Central to understanding human salvation, it is God's power at work saving the whole of creation by giving sinful persons the capacity to have faith and receive salvation through Christ.

Saints: Biblically, a saint is anyone who believes in Jesus Christ. In both the Old and New Testaments, saints refers to people who are dedicated and set apart for God.

the saved: Those who have accepted the Gospel message as truth and who have professed faith in Jesus Christ as the promised Messiah or Savior.

Scriptures: From the Latin word *scriptura*, meaning "writings." It refers to the Old Testament and New Testament inspired writings.

seal/seals believers: Kings in ancient times used a signet (often a ring) to confirm ownership of a document or object that could not be renounced or refuted, similar to the way animals are branded. The Holy Spirit seals believers into the family of God. God's Spirit is the believer's irrevocable proof of belonging to the household of God. The Holy Spirit guarantees that the salvation of believers is sure.

Second Advent/Second Coming: Christ's return to earth from heaven, as He promised. *John 14:3.* There are different interpretations of what will happen upon His return; however, there is no dispute that He shall return. See *1 Corinthians 15:52.*

seed (imperishable and incorruptible): Offspring, part of a recognized lineage. Born-again believers are adopted into the family of the eternal God and take on the quality of immortality.

Silas: An influential member of the early Christian Church who accompanied Paul on his second missionary journey. The two were miraculously released from jail by divine intervention after the Church prayed for their release. Silas is also believed to be Silvanus, mentioned in four of the New Testament epistles.

sin: Actions that rebel against the authority of God, fall short in obedience to God's commands, or "miss the mark." Human beings are born with a sinful nature, but also commit individual acts of sin. Sin separates us from God.

sin offerings: Sacrifices made during Old Testament days to restore a harmonious relationship with God. These offerings had to be made again and again. Jesus' death on the cross is the once-and-for-all sin offering for all who believe in Christ.

sin-converting power: The zeal some believers possess, empowered by the Holy Spirit, to express the Gospel message with such conviction and authority that others admit their sin and receive Jesus Christ as Lord and Savior.

Son of the Living God: Jesus. This phrase was first used by one of Jesus' disciples, Peter, when Jesus asked His disciples, "Who do you say that I am?" *Matthew 16:16*. This is the first indication that his disciples understood that Jesus was the Messiah, promised to the Jews, through whom God would provide salvation for all people. Son of the living God distinguishes the one true God from idol gods.

Souls (as in harvesting souls): Souls are lives. Harvesting souls is to show people how to gain eternal life through Jesus Christ. The Holy Spirit draws people to God, but Christians assist, thus the metaphor of Christians as harvesters of what God has made grow.

Spirit-baptized believer: Those who confess faith in Christ as Lord and Savior are given the Holy Spirit, the comforter promised by Jesus. Some faith traditions hold that Spirit baptism is evidenced by the believers speaking in tongues (unknown languages).

Spirit-filled believers: Followers of Jesus who empty themselves of personal pursuits and desires and let the Holy Spirit direct them in life matters.

spiritual gifts: The abilities given to believers to accomplish God's work on earth. Some distinguish natural talents from spiritual gifts, while others believe that talents are gifts to be used to build and expand God's kingdom on earth. *1 Corinthians 12:7* asserts that every believer is given a spiritual gift. See *Romans 12:6–8; 1 Corinthians 12:4–11, 28–31; Ephesians 4:7–13; 1 Peter 4:10.*

supernaturally: Attributable to a power that is far beyond human capacity. Throughout the Bible and human history, God has demonstrated divine power and authority in human events. These occurrences also may be deemed miracles.

tithes: Meaning "tenth," they are offerings back to God that reflects 10 percent of one's earnings. God's people are instructed to give back to God a tenth of what has been given to them by God. Abraham presented a tithe of war booty to Melchizedek, priest-king of Jerusalem. *Genesis 14:18–20.* Jacob pledged to God a tithe of all his possessions upon his safe return. *Genesis 28:22.* In *Malachi 3:8*, God equates the withhold of tithes to robbing God. Jesus, however, cautioned that strict tithing must accompany concern for demands of the law, such as for just and merciful living. See *Matthew 23:23, Luke 11:42*.

transgression: Sin; stepping beyond the limits of God's will and law.

translation: See **Bible translation**.

trespassers: Offenders; sinners. This term is used most frequently in the King James Version of the Bible to describe those who commit offenses against another.

tribulations: This term is generally used to describe various kinds of problems and troubles, either individually or as the body of Christ. In Revelation, the tribulation is a period of time when the Church will endure persecution and difficulties before the return of Christ. These difficulties are not sent by God, but rather those who oppose God. See *Revelation 7:14*.

the twelve apostles: The twelve persons who were an active and intricate part of Jesus' earthly ministry and who continued to spread His message after He went to heaven. The Bible confirms Jesus' relationship with twelve men who formed His inner circle. See *Matthew 10:1–4, Mark 3:13–19, Luke 6:12–16, John 6:67–72, Acts 1:26*.

the twelve tribes of Israel: The ancestry of the twelve tribes of Israel originates with Jacob (the grandson of Abraham), whose name was changed to Israel. Each of the tribes is named for one of Jacob's male progeny. See *Genesis 29:31–35, 30:1–13 and 19–24, 35:16–18, 41:50–52; Exodus 32:26–29; Joshua 13:33.*

ungodliness: Actions that are contrary to God's will, God's ways, or God's law; a denial of or disobedience to God.

voice of God: God reaches the mind and emotions of believers through the Holy Spirit. *1 Kings 19:11–13.* To connect with God, it is often necessary to block out the noise of the world.

volitional surrender: A voluntary surrender of the human will to obey God and follow Christ. God created humanity with the capacity to make choices, to follow Christ of our own free will.

wicked (noun, as in unbelievers): Those who do not accept Jesus as Savior and Lord. They will suffer judgment. The wicked dead of Revelation are the those who died without having accepted Jesus Christ as Savior and Lord.

will of God: God's blueprint for the created order. Although God has a divine will, God has created human beings with free will to choose divine will or not.

witness (verb), to witness: When believers spread the Gospel story, share the life and ministry of Jesus Christ, and give others the opportunity to attain eternal salvation through faith in Him.

Word of God: The Bible, which contains the promises, decrees, laws, and mandates of God.

worldly lusts: Uncontrolled behavior rooted in physical desires. Human beings are made up of mind, body, and spirit. Believers do not allow the urges of the body to dictate their thoughts and actions.

ABOUT THE AUTHOR

REV. DR. TERDEMA USSERY is a native of Gurdon, Arkansas, the oldest of five children. The family moved to Los Angeles in 1947, where they joined Emmanuel AME Church. Dr. Ussery graduated from Jefferson High School in 1949, then served in the U.S. Air Force from 1951 to 1955, attaining the rank of first sergeant.

Dr. Ussery and his lovely wife, Jean, met and married in 1956, and they recently celebrated their fifty-ninth wedding anniversary. They have two sons and a daughter, five grandchildren, and three great-grandchildren. Their elder son, Terdema II, is the former president and CEO of the Dallas Mavericks basketball team, and their younger son, Ian, is vice president in the Trust Department of a nationally known bank. Daughter Melody owns her own business, Stepping Stones, Inc., which services the needs of senior citizens and the mentally challenged.

Pastor Ussery, as he is so fondly referred to, earned a B.S. degree in business administration from Cal State University in Los Angeles, a J.D. from the South

Bay College of Law, and a master's degree in theology from Southern California School of Ministry. He holds a license in real estate. He worked in the Los Angeles Unified School District, taught adult education, and was a managing partner for the Slauson Farms Markets. He has served as the co-chairman of the Black-Korean Alliance Organization and chairman of the Committee Certifying Qualifications for ordination in the United Church of Christ, LA-Nevada Conference.

Jean and Terdema have served at the Emmanuel AME Church and Little Bethel United Holiness Church. They culminated their service to the Lord when they were called to co-pastor the Pilgrim United Church of Christ in Los Angeles from 1995 to 2006. Upon his retirement from Pilgrim and because of his outstanding leadership in the congregation, Pastor Ussery was conferred the illustrious distinction of pastor emeritus.

While at Pilgrim, Jean served as music director, director of youth ministries, chair of the women's fellowship, head of social outreach, and as an ordained deacon.

As a married couple, Jean and Terdema are truly one of God's dynamic duos! Jean united with the First Presbyterian Church of Inglewood in 2010 by transfer of membership, and Pastor Ussery has been serving as assistant to the pastor, while retaining his membership in the United Church of Christ as honorably retired.

WITH GRATITUDE FROM A BELIEVING SON

Dad had been working on this outline on and off for several years. Even so, it was still raw, unedited, and substantially incomplete when he showed it to me. It wasn't that it was an afterthought by any stretch of the imagination, but Dad would work on it whenever he had a spare moment or two, the result being that there was much left to be done. His life, however, was about to take a dramatic turn, and with it, this small but profound work would truly be birthed.

Both Mom and Dad have battled cancer the last three years. Mom successfully battled a fairly low grade of breast cancer, but Dad had a different and much more difficult fight looming. In Dad's case, he was diagnosed with the most aggressive form of prostate cancer in the summer of 2013. His Gleason and PSA scores were off the charts. He was stage 4. I asked an oncologist at UCLA Medical Center what would happen if, given Dad's age, we simply decided to do nothing. He replied,

"He'll be gone in about a year. This isn't a 'watch and wait cancer.'" So we pursued the only option available— hormone treatment followed by an aggressive radiation protocol. (Surgery? "He's too old, and given his scores, it's likely already spread." Chemo? "It's too late for that, and it would probably kill him before the cancer would naturally.") The senior oncologist treating Dad was very clear about his prognosis: "We can't cure this. You're too far along, and it's too aggressive, but my hope is to slow it down and get you a couple of years extra if we're lucky."

I promised Dad that I would try to come out to Los Angeles once a week to take him to his treatments at Kaiser Permanente Hospital (Hollywood), the very hospital where I was born decades ago. My brother and my uncle Wallace (Dad's only brother) had primary appointment duty. But I came in when I could, and candidly, it was difficult to watch the effects of radiation on Dad. He seemed to age a year for every week of treatment. After several weeks of treatment, his breathing quickly became labored, and he sweated profusely, could barely walk, and was hunched over like he had no spine. And that was after only a few steps.

I stopped asking Dad questions because it was too difficult watching him try to collect enough energy to answer. Indeed, a month before his radiation treatments ended, I was pulled aside by one of his physicians who said, "It's time for you to have a candid conversation with your father about the future. He is having a lot of complications. Given the dosages we are giving him already and the advanced stage of the cancer, the outcome may not be what we hoped it would be." The radiation was taking a severe toll.

I never initiated that conversation, but Dad did one evening with my uncle, my brother, and my son, Terdema III, in attendance. No longer comfortably able to speak, Dad laboriously told us what he wanted to happen when he passed. We made a collective vow to him that we would see his wishes through. He was visibly relieved.

And then we went back to the routine that had become commonplace during his illness: daily treatments at Kaiser combined with as much prayer as we could muster. His church family prayed. His biological family prayed. And he and Mom prayed. Our collective prayer? That God's will for his life be done. We knew that if God's purpose for Dad's life wasn't yet complete, his life would be spared. We prayed for a miracle in the context of that knowledge, while humbly acknowledging that it was in God's hands and was therefore going to be all right regardless.

A month or so after Dad's last treatment, I flew to Los Angeles to take him to his most critical appointment. We were going to be told the results of the treatment. My brother and I accompanied our parents to the doctors' office to hear the news. Given Dad's condition, we were apprehensive but also prepared for whatever God had in store. The senior oncologist specializing in prostate cancer and the senior urology resident crowded in the small room with us and delivered the following news: "There is no indicia of cancer. None. Your father is a medical mystery right now. We don't know if it's cured, which we told you we couldn't do, or just hiding, but we can't find anything. It is as if it never existed. So we will see you every six months just to check in on you, but there is currently nothing there." We were so stunned that no one said a word for a couple of minutes. And then, after thanking the doctors, we left.

Dad was quiet the whole night. In fact, the whole household was. One would think that, hearing such great news, the house would've been filled with celebratory chatter. But it was just quiet—as quiet as it had ever been. I had an early flight back to Dallas the next morning, so I knocked on my parents' bedroom door to say good night and goodbye. I also felt an overpowering need to deliver a simple message to Dad: "We don't know why you have been spared, but you have been. I hope you will take the time to get with God and ask Him what it is He wants you to do next. You are a 'medical mystery,' a 'miracle,' according to one doctor. There has to be a reason." Dad nodded knowingly.

Well, I sincerely believe that you are holding one reason in your hands right now. After regaining some strength, Dad immediately went to work on this outline, and here we are. This is not to suggest that this is the ONLY reason God has yet again shed His grace so generously on Dad. It IS to say, though, that this is at least part of the answer to the question "God, what's next?"

So what have I learned watching Dad? What benefit has there been in being raised in a home where Christ was the center? To be blunt, on a very personal note, I have to say that watching him live a life that is constantly gesturing toward the cross has been revelatory, motivating, and, indeed, life saving for me. Let me explain.

My siblings and I grew up in a 900-square-foot home in the Watts/Compton area of South Central Los Angeles. Our home was a few blocks from the notorious Nickerson Gardens housing project, directly around the corner from "Killer King" (i.e., Martin Luther King, Jr. Hospital). To this day, I can remember being a little boy watching my dad singlehandedly add on an additional 500 square feet—enlarging it to 1,400 square feet—so that he and Mom could have their own bed/bathroom, we could add a washer/dryer and eliminate the trips to the washteria, and expand the kitchen. Dad, the son of a carpenter, has always been good with a toolbox. His work ethic was trumped only by his insistence that we were in church on Sundays. That came first with him and Mom. And the lessons that we learned then ("Jesus is your friend" and "He will never leave or forsake you") are ones that still resonate today, some fifty years later.

I accepted Christ when I was thirteen years old. Bishop Fortier was preaching at a church in Watts, Little Bethel United Holy Church. During altar call, I made the walk up to the front that would forever transform my life. I unexpectedly left Compton a year later, at fourteen, on an academic scholarship, and things took off from there. I suppose that by any measure I have achieved some modicum of success: I have degrees from all three of the "Big Three" Ivy League Schools (i.e., Princeton, Harvard, and Yale), as well as one from the University of California at Berkeley Law School.

I served in the Chambers of two great men, Justice Allan Broussard of the California Supreme Court, and Chief Justice John Mowbray of the Nevada Supreme Court. Afterward, I practiced law at Morrison and Foerster, one of our nation's great law firms, representing institutions like Bank of America and the Industrial Bank of Japan, before getting into the business side of sports. I have been General Counsel of a professional sports league, Commissioner of a league, President of Nike Sports Management, and, for the past eighteen-plus years, President and CEO of the NBA's Dallas Mavericks. I then briefly served as President, Global Sports Categories, for a major footware and apparel company, Under

Armour. Recently, I resigned that position to take some much-needed time off.

Along the way, I have worked with some of the most prominent athletes in professional sports; worked with or alongside several billionaires; have traveled around the world multiple times; dined at the White House (a couple of times); dined with the royal family in Monaco; traveled with the "Dream Team"; won an Emmy or two; served on numerous for-profit and not-for-profit boards; received various honors and accolades; and have attained the "things" that our society seems to place so much value on these days.

In an age when our society most admires those who most admire themselves, I suppose there would be some benefit in being cautiously proud. There is a problem, though, as I believe that looking at these measures to determine a person's "worth" or "value" is tragically deceptive.

In sum, "what" I have achieved would probably be classified as "success" by the world. But I am smart enough to know that none of the aforementioned goes to "who" I am or "whose" I am. And who is that? I am a husband, father, brother, and son. At my core, I am simply a man under the cross like you, like those who came before me and those who will follow. I am a sinner, saved by the grace of God. And it is here, more than in any other way, that Dad's life has been a source of inspiration for me.

Part of what has made my journey so unique is that there were no role models in the home or community who could tell me what to expect at Princeton, or at a big law firm, or in business. I can still vividly remember standing outside of the Wells Fargo Tower in downtown Los Angeles the night before my first day on the job at Morrison. I had taken Dad there to show him my office on the forty-fourth floor. But he didn't want to go inside, so we stood on a darkened corner at the base of the building and talked. I wanted to show him where I was working to honor him. He appreciated that, but it was a foreign world and he wasn't comfortable going inside, even at night. When I asked if he had any advice he said, "Get a good secretary" and "keep God close."

I could give you a hundred stories where Dad, who to this day is my best friend, gave me simple but profound insight into "how" we are To LIVE as opposed to how we should go about MAKING A LIVING. They are obviously inextricably intertwined for believers, but I have found that over the years there were times when I lost sight of that, to my detriment. I have often called Dad for counsel and advice. He is a patient listener, but in the end, he always gets around to these words: "What does the book say, Lamar?"

In other words, the most enduring lesson Dad has taught over the years has been to reinforce, time and again, that irrespective of the particulars of the circumstance, the wisdom that God has made available to us through His word, in addition to His love, His grace, and His mercy, is always ALWAYS enough. No matter how crushingly painful, complicated, lonely or even tragic, God's promise that "I will never leave or forsake you" has rung true for me over these past five decades. This is worth remembering, not only in the bad times, but perhaps, most important, in the good. It is in the latter circumstances when we are most likely to forget the ubiquity and necessity of God's presence. He is omniscient, omnipresent, and omnipotent through good times and bad. We would do well to stay mindful of this truth.

It is often said that one of the few choices you cannot make in life is the identity of your parents. So we— my brother Ian, my sister Melody, and I—are grateful to God for having blessed us with the two who were preselected for us. We are also grateful that they are still actively with us today. It has been fascinating to watch them both as they have turned the final corner and are in the homestretch of their biological lives. The seasons of life dictate that the short days of our winter will one day come, and it has for them, as they are in their eighties now. My siblings and I are at an age where we have friends who have escorted their parents to death's door and whispered "until we meet again." We have not had to take that walk yet, although we are not naïve. That day is closer than ever.

We are thankful to God for our father and mother. Their lives have been ones of joyfully unselfish service in the home, the church, and the greater Los Angeles community. We have learned an enormous amount by simply observing them over the years. We got lucky. We drew the long straw in the parents sweepstakes!

We are honored that you have picked up this small but powerful book prepared by our dad. It is astounding. It is simple. It contains the truth.

We hope that through its contents you get an intuitive feel for Dad's ministry. Most important, we hope that, after spiritually absorbing its contents, you come away with a closer, more intimate walk with Christ.

Terdema Lamar Ussery II
Dallas, Texas
June 2016

NOTES

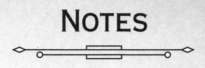

_____

_____

_____

_____

_____

_____

_____

_____

_____

_____

_____

_____